The Complete Cheapskate

The
Complete
Cheapskate

How to Get Out of Debt,
Stay Out, and Break Free from
Money Worries Forever

Mary Hunt

ST. MARTIN'S GRIFFIN ❧ NEW YORK

www.stmartins.com

All Scripture references are taken from the Holy Bible,
New International Version® (NIV)®.
Copyright © 1973, 1978, 1984 by
International Bible Society.
Used by permission of Zondervan Publishing House.
All rights reserved.

Portions of this book were originally published under the
titles *The Best of Cheapskate Monthly* and *The Cheapskate
Monthly Money Makeover*, both by St. Martin's Press.
The Complete Cheapskate was originally published
by Focus on the Family Publishing.

Articles in Appendix A and tips in Appendix B are
reprinted with permission of *Cheapskate Monthly*.
Copyright © 1992–2003, *Cheapskate Monthly*,
P.O. Box 2135, Paramount, CA 90723-8135;
(310) 630-6474.

Cheapskate Monthly® is a registered trademark.

ISBN 0-312-31604-6

5 7 9 10 8 6 4

*This book is lovingly dedicated
to the thousands of people who make up
the* Cheapskate Monthly *family.
You have encouraged me with your
loyalty, strength, and determination.
I consider it a privilege to walk beside you
on the path of financial solvency.*

CONTENTS

ACKNOWLEDGMENTS

I wish to thank the thousands of people who have written to me over the past twelve years. Your candor, courage, and progress reports have encouraged me more than you will ever know. Your enthusiasm and approval rates have annihilated my perceived personal limitations, and your willingness to share your personal financial struggles and remarkable progress has contributed to the success of *Cheapskate Monthly*.

Special thanks to my assistant, Cathy Hollenbeck, for her constant help, invaluable expertise, and loyal support; and to all the wonderful folks at St. Martin's Press for sharing my passion for this subject matter.

Special thanks to my wonderful husband, Harold, and sons, Jeremy and Josh, for their love and patience and for never complaining when the table is covered with books and manuscripts instead of dinner. I love you.

INTRODUCTION:
WHO ARE YOU CALLING
A CHEAPSKATE?!

I am certain that many of you are completely turned off by the term *cheapskate*. At first I was, too. But please hear me out. I had to come up with a term that implies the complete opposite of a spendthrift, and I think *cheapskate* fits the bill. Give it time—it will grow on you.

Let me explain what I mean by a cheapskate, and I think you'll agree it's a positive label. A cheapskate:

- does not spend more money than he or she earns, no matter how desperate or tempting the situation might appear
- has a spirit of generosity, regularly sharing money, time, and other resources with people in need
- lives honestly and ethically, regardless of the temptation to do otherwise in order to get a better deal
- saves at least 10 percent of all income

- does not buy compulsively but makes intelligent and well-thought-out choices
- lives within a financial plan that includes a margin for fun and spontaneity

That's it! Nothing negative or shameful. Being a cheapskate is honorable. You see, there is absolutely nothing wrong with having nice things or having dreams and goals for achievement and success. But we get into trouble when we demand the right to have things now by diving head over heels into debt through the improper use of credit. We also create problems for ourselves when we allow money and material possessions to dominate our thoughts and motivations.

A cheapskate, as I define it, is one who has a balanced, honest, and dignified approach to money management.

There is something else you must understand: There are two types of cheapskates. First is the natural-born kind. This is a person who is naturally thrifty and probably has never bounced a check, made a compulsive purchase, or taken on debt. I am in awe of you natural-borns, and please let the rest of us learn from you.

Second, there are the converted cheapskates. This is the category into which I—and most cheapskates—fall. Even though I was born into a thrifty family and grew up observing and living a frugal lifestyle, the lessons it did not stick. I must have been a natural-born spendthrift. But I am living proof that conversion is possible.

Cheapskates also have many different approaches. I do not personally advocate a bag-lady style. I don't collect cans along the beach or go through industrial dumpsters. But you should see me stretch a dollar at the grocery store. I don't cram my philosophy down anyone's throat or impose my personal style on family or friends. I like to think that I am a classy, dignified cheapskate.

For example, I would prefer one very nice outfit to ten from the thrift store. I would live frugally fifty weeks of the year to allow for a nice family vacation. I am more interested in finding effective ways to save cash—for example, by cutting medical and auto insurance costs, opening my own money-market account with $100, or learning how to keep my car in good repair for the least amount of money—than I am in saving egg cartons with the hopes of thinking up some meaningful use for them! The thought of buying a piece of income-producing property is far more exciting to me than recycling aluminum foil. But that's just me. Others have a different philosophy, and that's fine.

I am proud to be a cheapskate, and I'm excited to share this way of life with you. By the time you finish this book, you, too, will be proud to be called a cheapskate.

The Complete Cheapskate

BEEN THERE, DONE THAT: MY STORY

How I Went from
Spendthrift to Cheapskate

I used to be anything but a cheapskate. I broke into a cold sweat at even the thought of being considered cheap. And I was driven to make absolutely sure a clear line of demarcation was drawn between me in my world and those pitiful souls residing in the Land of Cheap. I charged my way through life feeling quite entitled because I had every credit card known to the English-speaking world.

It all started quite innocently with a promise. As a child, I was a daydreamer, a future-planner. I grew up embarrassed that I had to wear hand-me-down clothes and things purchased at the secondhand store. I, the Scarlett O'Hara of the fifties, vowed that I would never be poor and that my children would never wear clothes from the thrift shop. I declared that my children and I had "status," as if I could establish it by waving a magic wand. In fact, I had no idea how to achieve it.

Within days of my wedding, I cautiously suggested to my new

husband, Harold, that we look into getting a gasoline credit card. After all, now that we were married, we were entering a new social stratum, and every real family must be prepared for unforeseen emergencies. We needed to get with the program and stop depending on cash so much. We needed plastic! Harold went along with the idea, and before I knew it, we received two shiny new credit cards, one bearing my name. Wow! "Free" gas whenever I wanted it! No longer would I have to dig around for loose change in order to pump a few gallons into my car. I could fill up whenever the mood struck, and I knew that never again would I be concerned with mundane issues such as the price of gas. It felt good to carry clout. Being a married woman was quite prestigious.

Before long it seemed only logical that we should have an alternative brand of gas available (just in case we were away from our regular station), so we applied for a second set of credit cards. After all, if one was good, two would be better. We obtained the second set more quickly and with less effort than the first. I could feel our status soaring to new heights; I carried the proper credentials to prove it.

By the time our babies came along, the first credit card had been canceled by the gasoline company. We'd been late with some monthly payments and missed a few altogether. Now who would have thought a big company with all that money would demand that we pay it back, in full, every month? Not to worry, though. In addition to an assortment of gasoline cards, I'd added every department store card in southern California.

It was so easy. If a particular store didn't automatically send me preapproved cards in the mail, all I had to do was pick up an application in the store. It became a game, somewhat like collecting baseball cards. I was compelled to acquire credit cards— they gave me a sense of freedom and status. You must understand that I didn't apply for the cards with a specific purchase in mind;

rather, I wanted the security I believed they would bring us. I rationalized that we needed them in case of emergencies. Little did I know that the very things I thought would provide security were to become a catalyst for crisis.

Harold was soon promoted to middle management in a large, prestigious California bank. I couldn't have been prouder. One of the perks of his benefits package was an unsolicited bank card— with a very handy line of credit. Now not only was I "entitled" to all the gas I could use, but the department store cards and bank card prepared me for any unforeseen emergency. And unlike the gasoline companies, the others didn't require full payment each month. Instead, they were quite pleased to allow a small monthly payment. What's more, the companies all but pronounced a blessing over me every time I used their cards.

Soon I found my life filled with many little "emergencies." Often they arose from my poring over department store catalogs that showed up in the mail. My overactive mind and impulsive tendencies would join forces to convince me of an urgent need. I would become privately fixated on a certain item and be unable to relax until I found a way to get it. I felt a certain high, albeit temporary, when I bought the latest in kids' clothing or GI Joe action figures for my boys. I felt justified in spending huge sums in fabric stores. I would buy everything needed for project after project, telling myself I could make all kinds of clothes and decorator items for far less than the store-bought equivalents. In reality I completed few of the projects, and the materials became piles in the garage, destined to be included in the next Goodwill donation.

One of the best parts of being a cardholder was this: the more I used those credit cards and continued making the minimum monthly payments, the better standing and status the card companies bestowed on me. Why else would they keep increasing my limits? When the bank credit-card limit reached the four-figure mark, I just knew they thought I was fantastic. I was certainly keeping that promise I'd made to myself: I was not poor, and my kids did not wear clothes from the thrift store. We certainly *looked* good.

Shopping became even easier in the seclusion and comfort of my home. With a phone in one hand and a mail-order catalog in the other, I could create the windfall of Christmas for myself and my children anytime I had a whim. I realize now I was attempting to go back and fix my own childhood by giving my children all the clothes, toys, and attention I had missed. I was trying to fill a void by giving gifts that were bigger and better than the recipient could believe. I was making up for what I'd lacked, fulfilling my vow that my kids and I would never be poor and that I would always have the approval and the acceptance of my friends—even if I had to buy both. I lived out the only agenda I knew: External appearances are all-important. Anything going on inside myself that might conflict with my perfect facade must be ignored, denied, and put aside.

My instruments of entitlement were not limited to credit cards; I also had a checkbook. While I considered credit-card spending to be long-term deferment ("long-term" meaning I would pay hundreds of years later), writing checks was short-term deferment. Often I neglected to record the checks I wrote. It was safer that way because Harold couldn't track my spending. His tendency to be unobservant became my ally. I could all but redecorate the entire house, and he wouldn't notice.

I worked according to the philosophy that somehow, by the time the check was ready to clear, I would magically come up with funds I could sneak into the bank account. Of course, it rarely happened, but I still wrote checks, often with reckless abandon. One of two things happened over and over again: I either overdrew the account or brought the balance down so low that when Harold went to pay bills, the account no longer held enough to get us through the month.

Writing rubber checks would have been bad enough in any circumstances, but to make matters worse, Harold was the bank manager! Let me assure you that such behavior from employees is not looked upon kindly by your average financial institution. Imagine his embarrassment and rage when one of his staff members sheepishly advised him of the situation and suggested that he make an immediate deposit. The phone calls I received when that happened are memories I'd rather forget. And you think *your* blood runs cold when the bank calls!

More than once, my actions placed Harold's job in jeopardy, but I still couldn't stop my outrageous behavior. I was not making enormous purchases—certainly not new cars or expensive jewelry. Yet I was five-and-ten-dollaring us to death.

Inwardly I felt frail, weak, and insignificant. The act of spending gave me momentary sensations of power and strength. I temporarily felt cared for and nurtured—wonderful feelings that I made sure I experienced often.

As time went on, things got pretty sticky, especially around the first of each month. I had incurred such heavy consumer debt (all those credit accounts accruing interest at rates of 18 percent and up) that our monthly expenses exceeded our income. Fortunately for us—or so I thought—we were benefiting greatly from the real-estate boom of the seventies and eighties. Each time we got too far behind, we refinanced the house, pulling out our precious equity and plunging ourselves deeper and deeper into trouble. And, of course, the higher mortgage payments eventually put us right back where we'd been. We bought into the debt-consolidation theory: take out one big loan to pay off all the small ones and end up with a more manageable payment each month.

What a terrible mistake that was! Slowly but surely, the accounts paid off with the consolidation loan inched their way back up to the limit, and we were in worse shape than ever.

I was convinced that Harold's work in banking would never provide the level of income we needed to live our chosen lifestyle and that he should look at other career options—ones with big bucks available. So when an opportunity came along to try self-employment, he said good-bye to the bank, sixteen years of tenure, and regular paychecks. We took another financial plunge.

Together we made some crucial blunders. We were driven by the fantasy of getting rich quick, and we went blindly into a multilevel marketing-and-sales business that we knew nothing about. Worse, we did it with borrowed funds. It's no wonder that in only four months our first entrepreneurial endeavor ended in abrupt and devastating failure . . . and the loss of all the money we'd borrowed.

Our debts were enormous, and our income was nonexistent. Now both Harold and I were unemployed, and the anxiety and turmoil became unbearable. Seeing no way out of the mess, I became terrified and desperate. I'd run out of options and clever schemes to deal with emergencies. I felt like a magician with amnesia, a plate spinner with paralysis, a juggler who'd just had her arms amputated. I'd brought together all the elements that frequently prompt a divorce, bankruptcy, the loss of the home, and the destruction of the family. I felt that everything in my life was on the verge of meltdown. Only when I hit absolute rock bottom was I willing to consider change, no matter how radical. Finally I'd come to the place where I was willing to do anything to alleviate the most horrible pain I'd ever known.

I vividly recall that Saturday afternoon in 1982—the day I finally faced reality. I needed to get away to think things through, and I ended up at my in-laws' house. More than likely, I was looking for the kind of comfort and reassurance only parents know how to give, but that particular day no one was at home. Looking back, I see clearly that God needed to take me to his woodshed to teach me a hard lesson. What I needed was the truth—however painful—and not soothing words from parents telling me that everything would be okay.

At no time before or since can I remember feeling so hopeless. Sure, my faith in God was real. But I'd never depended on God when it came to finances. I trusted in my credit cards and in my own schemes more than in God's promises. That day, as I sat in the silence and emptiness of my in-laws' house, it was as if the floodlights of heaven illuminated the dark caverns of my life. For the first time I saw in living color the magnitude of the mess I'd made. I'd been deceptive, deceitful, and manipulative. I'd lied and cheated in order to have things my way. And I was certain that I'd all but destroyed my husband's life.

As I began to deal honestly with my situation, I asked for God's forgiveness and His help in rebuilding my life. As I prayed and poured out my problems and worries to God, I was comforted by reading the Bible.

There in the kitchen I fell to my knees and begged God's forgiveness for the horrible mess I'd created. I made a new promise: I would stop my irrational spending and debting, and I would do whatever it took to pay back whatever we owed. I asked God to help me change. I realized that I had far more control over my spending than I had ever wanted to admit. I could change my bad habits. I no longer had to convince anyone, including myself, that I wasn't poor.

I understood something else—though both Harold and I had made big mistakes, it was primarily *me* who had brought us to the point of financial (and emotional) ruin. I needed to start making major financial contributions to our marriage partnership. I had made far too many withdrawals.

Willing to do anything (fear is a great motivator), I accepted a full-time job that was offered to me about ten days later. Because I had earned my real-estate license, I was able to combine property management with sales, providing a steady income plus commissions. It was a good thing, too, because Harold decided he needed to stay home for a while. I became the breadwinner.

What a turn of events! We immediately eliminated all day-care costs. Two little boys got to spend huge amounts of time with their dad, and I was relieved of the pressure that many working moms experience, because Harold took over the household tasks. We switched roles, and it was awkward at first. But I adapted quickly. Being scared witless was probably the best thing that could have happened to me.

At the same time, we had to learn frugality—a new concept. It didn't come naturally by any means. However, we were shocked at how much we were able to cut back. The most amazing thing, though, is that no one, including the kids, really noticed our scaled-back standard of living. It just goes to show that others are not nearly as impressed with our artificial lifestyles as we think they should be.

Gradually, as we were able to reverse our spending habits, we began to get out of debt, and our drastically reduced living requirements became our way of life. Things went so well that in 1985 we were able to go into business for ourselves in a more practical and sensible way. With backgrounds in banking and real estate, we opened our own industrial real estate company.

If all of this sounds too easy, understand that I'm telling the condensed version of our story. Nothing happened overnight. In fact, it took us the next thirteen years to get completely out of debt.

While we did pay back every single dime of interest, penalties, and principal, the scars will be with us forever. We will always wonder what might have been had I not been so financially foolish. But one step at a time, we continue to make progress. And I am still learning that my dignity and self-worth do not come from possessions and that my self-image cannot be dependent on the number of credit cards I carry.

Thankfully, we didn't have to file for bankruptcy, we didn't lose the house, and, best of all, our marriage has been strengthened by the tremendous challenges we've faced. We learned to save money, and our two sons have grown into fine young men who have learned financial responsibility right alongside us.

After struggling for ten years not only to make ends meet every month but also to make significant repayments toward the massive debts I had run up, in October 1991 I became impatient with the snail's pace of our progress. My impatience drove me to think of some way I could increase our income in order to get this repayment thing over and done with—and quickly! We had better things to work for, and, quite frankly, I was tired of living with monthly reminders of the pathetic mistakes I'd made.

Trying my hand at writing a newsletter seemed like a good idea. I certainly had a timely topic, lots of material, and lessons from the school of hard knocks. Since I already had an office established, I was pretty much set up to start another business. The writing part was an unknown, but I felt confident enough to at least give it a shot. Having mastered the effective business letter, I figured a newsletter would have some of the same characteristics.

So on January 1, 1992, *Cheapskate Monthly* premiered. It received a surprisingly positive response from readers across the United States and Canada. Today, our fifty thousand subscribers, both through the mail and online (www.cheapskatemonthly.com), continue to learn that with a little ingenuity, perseverance, and determination, they can live within their means without sacrificing their dignity or quality of life.

God has taken the mistakes and blunders in my life and begun to weave a tapestry of unbelievable beauty. I cannot express how thankful I am.

Cheapskate? Who, me? You bet!

2

ARE YOU A GOOD MONEY MAKEOVER CANDIDATE?

Diligence, Not Miracles, Brings Results

Makeovers. Wonderful, aren't they? Someone waves a magic wand and—*poof!*—everything that was unattractive is miraculously new and gorgeous.

My favorite makeovers are the ones featured on television shows, because I don't have to wait for the results. Through the miracle of TV, I get to see the pathetic "before" at the beginning of the show and the sensational "after" at the end. I do exactly what the show producers hope I will: I watch the entire show just to see the makeover result. Call me sentimental, but I actually cried when an unsuspecting lady of the house opened the door of her home and revealed a complete decorating makeover, compliments of daytime TV's most popular talk show. She cried, and I cried along with her (mostly out of jealousy, I'm sure). They spent big bucks to make sure it was a successful show, and the ploy worked.

Makeover—an amazing word that says, "You aren't looking

that great. You could use some improvement. You need help. I can fix you." But not every face or every home needs a makeover. Imagine the lunacy of a popular magazine offering to do a makeover on Cindy Crawford or a home improvement show calling the White House to offer its services.

There is one kind of makeover, however, that most people could benefit from—a Money Makeover. How about you? Are you a hopeless case, or are you in such good shape that a money makeover would not only be useless, but an insult to your fine money-management skills? If you are experiencing joy and an absence of stress, if the few bills that you do have are paid on time, if you are not rolling over debt from one month to the next, and if you feel well prepared for the future, congratulations! You really don't need a Money Makeover. In fact, you should get in that other line with Cindy Crawford.

But the fact that you picked up this book leads me to believe that you might welcome improvement. Perhaps you need only a minor adjustment to get yourself back on track. Or maybe you have been derailed and require more-intensive work to get yourself rolling again.

Basically, all you need to qualify for a Money Makeover is *desire* and *capacity*. If you are ready to get your finances under control, relieve the stress money has created, and prepare for the future, then you are more than qualified in the desire category. If you earn money (no matter how much or how little) and are obligated to pay bills, you also have the capacity.

Situations That Call for Action

Following are some real and recurring financial situations. See if any of these scenarios sound familiar to you.

SITUATION NUMBER 1: You get an income-tax refund because you generously overpaid the government last year, asking the IRS to keep what it needs and send you the balance sometime after April 15—without interest, of course. Since you can't decide whether to put the money toward an outstanding debt or replace your beyond-repair washing machine, you "wisely" put the money into your checking account so you won't be tempted to spend it. A month or so later, you decide the washing-machine replacement idea has moved from optional to obligatory. You check your current checking account balance and are flabbergasted when you realize that the money is gone! (This prompts a few cross words with your spouse, since this kind of thing is always the *other person's* fault.) Somehow the entire tax refund has been absorbed into your everyday living expenses. Since you need a washing machine and you no longer have the cash that would have allowed you to consider a good used machine, you reluctantly go ahead and purchase a new one on credit.

SITUATION NUMBER 2: Things have been going well for a while, and for the first time in a long time, you actually have a few bucks left at the end of the month. You decide to go ahead and get the new patio furniture you've been eyeing. No sooner is the beautiful set delivered than your car breaks down. There's no way you could have predicted this, but the prognosis is not good. You need major repairs that are going to cost more than $600. Another crisis! Since you have no excess cash in the checking account and no savings, you have no choice but to go to the bank and take a cash advance on your credit card. This emergency is so dire that you don't even worry about the interest rate.

SITUATION NUMBER 3: You've been planning a family vacation. You really need to get away, and the kids are excited.

You've been meaning to start saving for the trip, but something seems to come up every month. Before you know it, it's time to make the reservations, and you don't have a dime set aside for the vacation. You rationalize that family time is a priority and that this trip is a once-in-a-lifetime opportunity, and besides, you work hard and you deserve a vacation just like all of your friends and coworkers. Now is certainly not the time to worry about the cost of things. You want to show the family a good time. You decide to put the trip on your credit card, but you promise yourself you'll make huge payments when you get home to pay it off quickly. (How many times have you said *that* before?)

SITUATION NUMBER 4: You've lived in your house for seven years (could it possibly be that long?) and still don't have living room furniture. The master bedroom looks the same as it did the day you moved in and will look gorgeous as soon as you get a little extra cash to decorate. You have plans. You know exactly how you want to decorate and furnish those rooms . . . just as soon as you get some extra money. Weeks, months, and years keep flying by, and still no extra money. You are embarrassed about how the place looks, so you seldom invite guests. Every time you visit a friend's home, you feel pitiful and envious and leave feeling unhappy about your own house.

SITUATION NUMBER 5: You carry a $250 deductible on your auto insurance in order to get the lower semiannual premiums. Wouldn't you know it? The one and only time you forget to look behind you before backing out of the grocery-store parking lot, you smack into a stupid little pole. You hit it so hard that you ram the rear fender right into the rear wheel. Total repairs: $1,200! You just don't have an extra $250 for the deductible, but your car is not drivable. What choice do you have? Your credit cards are all maxed out. Financial disasters don't often give a warning, so how in the world were you supposed to plan ahead? You are forced to go to your parents. They reluctantly spring for the cash, but you know what's going to happen. You are surely in for another lecture, and until you pay them back, you are going to feel guilty. The last time you borrowed from them, they made you feel like a little kid again. You just hate doing this, but what alternative do you have? You can't live without a car.

SITUATION NUMBER 6: You just moved into a new apartment, one with lots of windows and daylight. You are thoroughly ashamed of your living room furniture, which you realized was a bit tired in the old place but has suddenly dropped to horrible in its new surroundings. You happen to read an ad in the newspaper announcing a going-out-of-business furniture sale. You drop in just to see what they have and drop out an hour later with a nifty easy-payment contract in your pocket. You are tickled with how easily you were able to arrange financing on an eight-piece collection with classic French styling in the tradition of master European craftsmen. Who cares what the financing charges are? You were able to pull off the deal with no money down!

SITUATION NUMBER 7: You have a secret that is eating you alive. You have run up nearly $12,000 in credit-card debt during the last year alone, and your wife is completely ignorant of the fact. You handle the family finances, and while it's been tough, you've been able to juggle them well enough to keep her from finding out about the debt. When you took a slight pay cut last year, getting a few new preapproved credit cards seemed like a prudent thing to do—just in case. You didn't mention them to your wife because you knew she would just worry more about the money situation, and she depends so much on your ability to handle the finances. You didn't intend to start using the cards, but they seemed so available, and with the household funds being so tight temporarily (the company promised to restore your pay rate as soon as possible), paying for things with the cards did seem like the best way. A year later your salary has not increased, but your debt has. You've arranged to have the bills sent to the office, and creditors are starting to call you at work because you just can't keep up with those payments. You're scared to death that your wife or boss will find out. The only way out is to apply for more loans just to keep the minimum monthly payments current.

If you identified with any of these situations, you will benefit from a Money Makeover. I want to show you how to handle your money so that these situations (which can happen to anyone) won't disrupt your life. I want to teach you how to prepare for them, how to rework your finances so that you can relax and enjoy life. I'm even going to convince you to get out of debt. And I'm going to show you how to do it quickly—not in the so-slowly-that-you-will-pay-lots-of-interest way your creditors have in mind.

Are you still not convinced that a Money Makeover should be in your future? Grab a pencil and take the following miniquiz. Simply answer yes or no:

1. I spend much of my take-home income paying credit-card bills.

2. I am near, at, or over the limit on my lines of credit.

3. I am regularly late paying my bills.

4. I often must pay late penalties.

5. I make only the minimum payment on my charge account.

6. I have to pay half my bills one month and half the next month because I can't pay all of them at the same time.

7. I write postdated checks.

8. I've bounced three checks in the last year.

9. I often "overshop" to meet the minimum-purchase requirement for credit-card transactions.

10. I've taken a cash advance on one credit card to make the payment on another card.

11. I have to work overtime just to meet my current financial obligations.

12. I don't know exactly how much I owe in installment debts.

13. I worry about money quite a bit.

14. I do not have a regular savings program.

15. I carry a balance from month to month on at least one credit card and keep hoping to pay it off completely.

16. Some months I do pretty well, but other months I'm caught off guard by unexpected expenses.

17. I live from paycheck to paycheck and would be in big trouble if I lost my job.

18. I'd love to make charitable contributions, but it's impossible. There's just not enough money to go around. I am my own favorite charity.

19. I believe that if I made more money, I'd be just fine.

20. Creditors are calling all the time, and I just don't know how long I'll be able to juggle everything.

21. I use credit cards to buy things I would never purchase with cash.

22. I have applied for more than five credit cards in the past year.

23. I regularly pay for groceries with a credit card because I just don't have the cash.

24. My credit cards make me feel secure. I get a sense of freedom from my ability to charge things.

25. I have lied to my spouse or creditors about making payments.

If you answered no to all of the foregoing, you obviously know how to control your spending and manage your resources in an intelligent and reasonable manner. If you answered yes to three or fewer statements, you are probably okay for now, but you should consider this a warning sign. Unless you change your ways, problems do lie ahead for you. A Money Makeover is probably the best thing you could do to stop heading downhill.

If you answered yes to four or more statements, stick with me, kid. Keep reading this book, and you'll learn how to get out of this mess.

You're Not Alone

To reassure you that you are not alone, let me share some of the information I have gleaned from researching money matters and corresponding with the thousands of people who have written to me in the past several years. Ninety percent of your friends and relatives know very little about money management. Eighty percent of all Americans have never had a savings account, and only 10 percent of the total population has any idea how to control their spending.

As of this writing, there are *1,156,200,000* active revolving-balance credit cards in this country. Statistics indicate that only 32 percent of these cardholders pay their balances in full every thirty days. That means more than 786 million credit-card accounts carry balances month after month, year after year. This figure represents millions of people who are hopelessly doomed to live their lives imprisoned by *perma-debt*. (*Perma-debt* is that dreadful condition brought about by revolving debt, which rolls over from month to month, year to year, decade to decade, following its victim right to the grave.)

So why do so few people actually do something about their financial woes? Partly because a major characteristic of human nature is laziness. Many people are looking for a no-effort way to make their lives perfect. They want someone to fix their problems. Believe it or not, I've found that a great majority of the people in the worst financial trouble are willing to remain miserable until they win the lottery or are surprised by a big inheritance. While waiting, they continue to live in misery, limping through life, complaining all the way.

Many Americans have gotten into the bad habit of demanding "it" now and paying for "it" later. We have learned to feel entitled, and we think nothing of accepting "thirty-six easy payments" and a myriad of other marketing ploys. I hope that, not too many more pages into this book, you will be convinced that living this way is not going to do anything but keep you headed in a downward spiral—a killer spiral of uncontrollable debt and bondage.

Many people sincerely want to do something about their out-of-control financial situations but don't know how. Where do they go to find practical, affordable, and effective help? For those in major crises, there are twelve-step programs, credit-counseling organizations, and bankruptcy protection. But most people have not reached the point of requiring such intensive and dramatic intervention. A reasonable alternative is a Money Makeover.

If you are lazy and have no intention of working at your own makeover, you will not be successful because—I promise you—there are no miracles and no magic that will help you. But I can promise that if you carefully follow this plan, you will experience remarkable results. You know how lousy your "before" picture looks. Just wait to see how good your "after" picture will be!

3

Developing Healthy Money Attitudes

Progress Begins with Transforming
Your Heart and Mind

Regardless of your present financial situation, and regardless of the subtle or subconscious roles money has played in your life, you are not destined to live one more day under the control of your current money attitudes. The way that you have handled your money up to this point is probably the result of learned behaviors. I don't know about you, but I received absolutely no education on the simple matter of money and its role in my life, so it's no wonder I just played it by ear and did what came naturally.

Now you have a choice. Either you can continue with the bad habits that have landed you in need of a Money Makeover, or you can replace them with new, effective, and far more appropriate attitudes. In fact, developing healthy attitudes toward money is the first step to finding financial freedom and peace of mind. You can learn all the money-saving strategies and budgeting principles, but if you don't transform the underlying beliefs and perspectives that drive harmful financial practices, you won't make any *lasting* changes.

Let me make this perfectly clear: No matter how much you feel dominated by money, no matter how addicted you think you are to using your credit cards and to overspending, you have the ability to stop this outrageous behavior. You are not powerless over money's force in your life. You have the ability to make choices and control your actions. And you *can* change your actions anytime you set your mind to it. By repeating a new action over and over again, you will change your attitudes. And when your attitudes change, your behaviors change, and new actions become automatic. Researchers tell us that it takes three weeks—just twenty-one days—to create a new habit, and another three weeks to establish it for a lifetime.

As your attitudes about money change, something remarkable will happen. You will learn what truly constitutes abundance, and you will come to enjoy financial ease—not necessarily wealth, but contentment and a sense of well-being. You will see the focus of your life change from financial chaos to serenity and fulfillment.

Following are ten healthy attitudes about money. I have written them in the first person so that as you read them, they will immediately become personal.

NEW ATTITUDE NUMBER 1: *I choose to understand the truth about money.* I know that money cannot be equated with love, happiness, worth, respect, social standing, approval, acceptance, or goodness, nor can it purchase any of these things for me.

Money is simply a valuable commodity with which I am compensated for the use of my abilities, skills, and talents. Money is a convenient form of exchange for goods and services. It provides a means to a worthy end for me and for my family. I can abuse money, or I can put it to good use. I acknowledge that as money flows into my life, my responsibility will increase, because from the person to whom much is given, much is required.

Now that I've gotten it through my thick head exactly what money can and cannot do, I am free to find genuine and lasting sources of happiness, joy, approval, peace, and goodness.

NEW ATTITUDE NUMBER 2: *I commit to being responsible and honest.* I acknowledge that it is irresponsible to write checks before the funds are in my account, make purchases on credit when I know I don't have the resources to repay the debt immediately, fail to balance my checking account, not work up to my abilities, and put off paying my bills. I further acknowledge that it is dishonest to mislead my creditors, fail to pay my taxes, hide my purchases, and conceal my debts from my spouse. I commit to a new way of life, one of total integrity in which I refuse to spend more money than I have. Now I will respond openly and honestly in all of my financial affairs.

NEW ATTITUDE NUMBER 3: *I will not spend money that is not mine.* I commit to incurring no more unsecured debt (credit cards, personal loans, and so on). I won't borrow from a friend, accept a service that I will pay for later, take a loan from a bank, charge anything on any credit card that cannot be repaid immediately, or in any way pledge future income for present goods and services. No one can force me to go one more cent into debt.

NEW ATTITUDE NUMBER 4: *I will respond appropriately.* In the past I have used money inappropriately to make myself feel good, reverse bad moods, kill the pain of disappointment, make up for losses, feed my empty heart, fill my loneliness, anesthetize my sadness, and try to gain love and approval. Not only have I failed to deal with the real issues in my life, I have ended up with a pile of debts.

From now on when I encounter discouragement, stress, disappointment, or loneliness, I will not spend money in an effort to avoid facing the real, underlying problem. Instead, I will face the situation head-on and deal with the issues in a healthy way, which will cause me to grow and will not put my solvency at risk.

NEW ATTITUDE NUMBER 5: *I accept the responsibility and reject the shame.* I acknowledge that I am responsible for my present financial situation. I have made some mistakes. I have failed to plan ahead appropriately. But I am not the sum of my debts; my bank balance does not define who I am, and my creditors do not own me. I owe them money, which I will repay, but I do not owe them my life. No matter how painful or troubled my past has been, it is my *past.* I can learn from my past mistakes and will use the past only to motivate me to forge new financial territory. I am now facing the future joyfully and hopefully, and I am looking forward to solvency.

NEW ATTITUDE NUMBER 6: *I commit to clarity.* I acknowledge that because I have no idea where my money goes, I have allowed it to disappear. As part of my process toward solvency, I commit to recording the simple *details* of how I spend my money. I commit to facing the truth on a daily basis by keeping my purchases recorded, my checkbook balanced, my mail opened, and my bills in order and paid on time.

NEW ATTITUDE NUMBER 7: *I will realize my dreams.* This is my life. It is not a dress rehearsal. I refuse to defer living life to its fullest until some future time when I get my money situation straightened out. Without my dreams, my recovery will be bleak at best. I am confident that combining my life's work with my dreams will be a source of genuine happiness and, in turn, will bring success.

NEW ATTITUDE NUMBER 8: *I will search out true sources of happiness and will practice thankfulness.* I acknowledge that true happiness is found in the infinitely precious things that cannot be taken from me. I will look for my joy and contentment in what is permanent, and I will find my anchor in the fact that the God of the universe loves and cares for me. As I see the bigger picture, my day-to-day money issues will diminish and pale in the light of what is truly important.

For me it is impossible to feel self-pity and gratitude at the same time. The best way I can let go of worry and self-pity is to practice thankfulness. I will create my own personal and specific thankfulness list. I will begin thinking in terms of the blessings that money cannot buy, such as my faith, family, friendships, health, and freedom.

My thankfulness list will become something permanent and precious in my life. During the down times (which will inevitably visit me from time to time because I am human), I will reach for my constantly growing thankfulness list instead of the credit cards.

NEW ATTITUDE NUMBER 9: *I will regularly share my resources with others.* Recognizing that all I have is given to me by God, I commit to giving back a portion of my money to his work and to sharing my resources with those who are in need. I will do so joyfully and wisely, knowing that I am entrusted with resources and charged with the responsibility to use them to help others. I will give out of obedience and gratitude, not expecting anything in return.

NEW ATTITUDE NUMBER 10: *I commit to doing whatever it takes and to making whatever sacrifices are necessary to achieve and maintain solvency.* I understand that desperate situations often require drastic measures. I am willing to make the adjustments necessary to live within my means. My goal is to achieve personal solvency—that condition in which I give generously, save consistently, pay my bills, fulfill my obligations, and still have some left over.

Making commitments to these ten new attitudes all at once may seem overwhelming, especially if your situation is dire. But I promise that if you make this commitment, I will walk with you through the entire process, step-by-step. You will find yourself forming new money habits along the way.

Ask God for the wisdom and ability necessary to change your heart and behaviors in the area of your personal finances. As you seek His wisdom and guidance, He will transform your unhealthy attitudes into healthy ones.

4

THE DEBT MESS

*How You Got Here and How
to Begin Getting Out*

No one is born in debt. I suppose the day may come when each baby who comes into the world will be weighed, measured, fingerprinted, given a Social Security number, and assigned a portion of the national debt. I am thankful that the day has not yet arrived. The bad news is that most of us don't need the government to plunge us into debt—we manage to do that on our own.

If you are an average American, you have four credit cards. These plastic cards have become the standard passport into the vast world of shopping centers, mail-order catalogs, online shopping, restaurants, travel, and now even fast food joints and grocery stores.

For some reason, we have come to accept that if a credit-card application is approved, the amount of the credit limit becomes cash we're entitled to. If an auto loan is approved, it's as if a mandate has come from on high assuring us that this is certainly an affordable purchase. (It made sense to me. Why would the bank or credit company approve my loan if they didn't know I could repay it? After all, they're the experts.) We are a nation controlled by debt. As of this writing, overall consumer debt in the United States totals more than $878,535,000,000. This is nonmortgage debt. If you include mortgages, then the total is well over $1 trillion, a sum that exceeds the annual economic output of some nations.

Americans from all economic walks of life are sinking into their own black holes of debt, going into hock for everything from Baccarat crystal to breakfast cereal. The average American *household* has 11.5 active credit cards (not including debit or check cards). As a result, the average credit-card debt for Americans who carry balances reached an all-time high of $5,610 in 2000, an increase of one-third since 1995. As consumers struggle, credit-card companies such as Providian and First USA are making bigger profits than ever. Between 1995 and 1999, thanks in part to aggressive marketing and misleading practices, credit-card companies' profits nearly tripled, jumping from $7.3 billion to $20 billion.*

So what exactly is *debt*? Debt results when one person owes money to another person, place, or thing. In the strictest sense of the word, owing "a cup of sugar" or "your deepest gratitude" could be construed as a debt; hence the phrase "I am indebted to your generosity." But for the sake of this book, we'll limit our discussion to *monetary* debt.

Monetary debt comes in two forms—*secured* and *unsecured*. A secured debt involves something tangible to which the lender holds ownership until the debt is completely paid. This tangible property, also called collateral, is typically real estate or auto-

---

*Figures taken from www.CardFacts.com, CardWeb.com Inc., Frederick, Maryland, and Massachusetts Public Interest Research Group, www.truthaboutcredit.org.

mobiles. An unsecured debt is based upon the signature or promise of the borrower. Paying for clothes with a credit card results in an unsecured debt. If you fail to make your credit-card payment, the clothes police do not come out and repossess the articles.

For all practical purposes, secured debt is safe debt and not the subject of this chapter. Unsecured debt got me into trouble. This kind of debt controls the lives of millions of families and individuals in this country.

The difference between secured and unsecured debt has nothing to do with honor, intent, or good faith. Certain circumstances occur over which we have no control, such as sudden unemployment, prolonged illness, or the unexpected need of a friend or family member. In the case of a failure to repay a secured loan, or a safe debt, the lender retains ownership of the secured property, and the loan is considered repaid. In the case of unsecured debt, the creditor is out of luck. Your promise to pay is worthless, and he is left with no choice but to come after your credit rating.

Excellent financial principles are like the laws of nature—they remain universal and do not change through the ages. To "let no debt remain outstanding" has always been the preferred way to live; that's because the borrower is always the slave to the lender. Unsecured consumer debt places the debtor in bondage, and as the amount of debt increases, the shackles become tighter and heavier. We only deceive ourselves when we acquire goods and services through the use of credit cards and unsecured loans. We pretend that these purchases liberate us and make our lives fuller. The truth is that we just dig a pit, then jump in and cover ourselves with the weight of the debt. While we would be quick to concur that our heart's desire is to provide an income stream for the future, we are doing just the opposite.

We spend every cent we have, and when there isn't enough (perhaps every month!), the credit cards bridge the gap. For the

68 percent of people who don't pay off their credit-card balances every month, the debt begins to build. The next month something unexpected happens, and again the credit cards become lifesavers. Before long, making the minimum payments becomes more and more burdensome, requiring some other creative financing plan such as a debt-consolidation loan or another credit card.

Do you see what is happening here? We pledge *future* income—yet unearned—for *current* expenses. Then it becomes next year's salary that will be required to pay this year's expenses. The income of the next decade will likely be required to cover the expenses of the current decade!

Debt doesn't always come in the form of four- or five-figure loans. I incurred most of our debt a tiny bit at a time: a new outfit here, a nice dinner there, a weekend away because we "deserved" it, cash advances to cover unexpected car repairs . . . and on it went.

In fact, for most people, going into debt starts trivially and innocently with just a few dollars owed to a friend or family member. Next comes a credit card. Tiny little balances don't seem to be a problem. That $250 stereo is nothing more than $10 a month. Then come another card and a few minor emergencies. Before long, the debting becomes routine, a pattern that cannot be reversed in a single month.

COMMON WAYS DEBT IS INCURRED

- Taking a cash advance on a credit card
- Purchasing fuel with a gasoline card
- Requesting an advance on your paycheck, bonus, or commission
- Paying for meals with a credit card

- Putting airline tickets on a credit card
- Buying mail-order or online items with a credit card
- Failing to pay the rent on time (you owe it, so a debt is created)
- Making arrangements with a hospital, doctor, or dentist to make payments for services rendered

Nothing on the above list seems excessive or unusual, does it? Millions of people "debt" in these and similar ways, week in and week out. What's more, we are encouraged to do so. Most of us are pressured on a daily basis to buy on credit and to accept new credit cards and unsecured loans.

Several years ago, when we paid off another of our many department-store credit cards, I got a private moment of glee imagining the horror on the face of the computer operator who entered that last payment. I'm sure panic spread through the department when it finally sank in that for the first time in twenty-two years the Hunt account showed a zero balance.

My fantasy turned to reality when two weeks later we received two brand-new gold cards from this store with a new-and-improved credit limit of $2,150. The letter from the company's president applauded our most-favored standing! Not only did the store send the new cards, but the credit officers offered a 25 percent discount on the first purchase made with one of the cards and, in addition, "a lovely gift." They're no dummies—they know that if they can get me to use the gold cards once, chances are I'll be hooked again, and they can rest easy. I hope they can get over their disappointment.

When our son Jeremy graduated from high school, an exciting piece of mail arrived in our mailbox. Imagine how proud he was to be notified that he had been preapproved for a Visa card. The only thing required was his signature. The bank offering the card painted a solemn picture of the young man away at college with an emergency of dire proportions. The conclusion of the sales pitch was: "Now that you're going to be away from home, you need to be prepared to face life's little emergencies." The letter went on to point out how expensive books and supplies can be, and how comforting it is to know that you can eliminate worry by simply accepting the credit card. It sounded so wholesome, wise, and mature to plan ahead and be prepared for any predicament that might arise. Yes, it's wise to plan ahead, but plunging oneself into debt is not the way to do it.

WARNING SIGNS
OF IMPENDING FINANCIAL DOOM

- Not paying bills on time
- Writing the checks but waiting to mail them
- Rarely balancing the checking account
- Taking cash advances on credit card accounts
- Accepting additional credit cards
- Paying only the minimum on charge accounts
- Bouncing checks
- Borrowing from family and friends

If you are in debt, it probably didn't happen overnight. And getting out won't happen overnight either. I challenge you to resolve right now that you will not debt even one more dollar. Ever. I can't tell you that it will be easy, but I know you can do it. Clearing away the dark clouds of debt will release joy, passion, and excitement in your life.

Peer Pressure

Haven't you always considered peer pressure to be something that plagues only children and adolescents? Harold and I have always tried to teach our boys that peer pressure, if not recognized, could persuade them to participate in unwise or destructive behaviors only because "everyone else is doing it." We want our children to demonstrate control over the pressure of their peers, and we feel they should be able to weigh and measure options and make the right choices based upon their own value system. We tell them to stand up for what they know is right; the fact that everyone else is doing wrong doesn't mean they have to.

Such training is probably not effective if kids see their parents trying to "one-up" and keep up with their friends and peers. Have you ever considered that you might be accepting behaviors from yourself that you'd never tolerate in your kids? Many adults succumb to peer pressure, only they do so in different ways than young people. Just think of all the ways our lives are shaped and defined by peer pressure: how and where our kids are educated; the size and location of our homes; the model and year of our automobiles; the labels on our clothing; the magnitude and originality of birthday parties; the lavishness and immensity of Christmas; and on and on. . . .

Depending on your motivation, nothing may be wrong with these things in and of themselves; the problem occurs when debting becomes the only way to acquire goods and services and when peer pressure justifies the act.

Perma-debt

Issuers of credit cards have only one agenda: to keep us permanently in debt. Their mission is to put out the bait (the preapproved card), jerk the hook (offering an attractive interest rate, rebate, or gift on the first use), and reel us in. The rest is easy. They know that if the average person can be enticed to accept a credit card and use it just once, he or she will remain hooked for fifteen years or more.

Consumer-credit interest rates are sky-high—anywhere from, say, 9.9 percent to 26 percent. Companies have become so competitive that they like to snatch customers by offering teaser rates as low as 0 percent. But *beware!* Such rates are short-lived, automatically bump to higher rates, and include all kinds of provisions in the fine print that may be difficult to comply with. Late fees of $29 or higher, plus over-limit fees and punitive interest rates, kick in if a payment is ever late. If we take into account an annual fee, an over-limit fee, a cash-advance fee, and many other fees, some cards are effectively charging more like 30 percent interest. When you think in these terms, it's pretty hard to understand why anyone thinks that being a cardholder is a privilege.

Consumer credit is a big-time industry. The credit-card companies and banks have much at stake. Your perma-debt situation is their lifeblood, and you can be sure they are quite interested in maintaining that condition.

SHOULD YOU CUT UP
ALL YOUR CREDIT CARDS?

It would be wonderful not to carry any credit cards—then the means through which most debt is accumulated would be eliminated. But in these high-tech, electronic times, every family needs one all-purpose credit card (only one!). It will come in handy if you need to rent a car, secure a hotel room, or book airline tickets over the phone or the Internet. However—*and listen carefully*—the balance *must* be paid off during the grace period, or the activity turns into debting, and you know how dangerous that is.

If you don't trust yourself to carry a credit card, try this: Fill an empty coffee can half-full with water and freeze it. Then place your credit card on top of the ice and fill the can to the top with water and return it to your freezer. The card will be available if you *absolutely* need it, but the time required to thaw your ice-cube card will make it difficult to use and at least will give you time to reconsider any purchase you want to make with it.

Bouncing Checks

A checking account can be a clever way to acquire things when you're broke. I used to do it, so I know the difference between an honest mistake and a planned, contrived manipulation. Passing bad checks is against the law. Criminal prosecution is generally reserved for habitual offenders or people with criminal intent. If these criteria don't apply to you, chances are you don't need to worry about being jailed for it. Instead, you get to pay huge punitive damages. As of this writing, $30 a pop per bounced check is not unusual in many areas.

The way I see it, overdraft penalties are unconscionably large interest rates on money borrowed for a short period of time. Another problem arises, however, for the perpetual check bouncer: creditors and merchants don't trust people who bounce checks.

If you have never had a problem with bouncing checks, you're to be admired. If, on the other hand, you have experienced this problem firsthand, you've probably felt the shame that goes along with it. The whole concept of the checking account was developed to fulfill a need for convenience and safety—not to be used as a loan vehicle. If you know the embarrassment of having an account closed involuntarily due to excessive overdraft activity, you would do well to heed my advice and do whatever it takes to change your ways. Here are some tips:

- *Record every transaction.* I can almost hear some of you checkbook-perfectionist types laughing, "But many of us have difficulty doing this." You see, once the expenditure is written down, it becomes real. Until such time, a state of denial can be quite comfortable. As long as the current balance remains a guesstimate, you feel as if you can continue spending with reckless abandon. It's amazing how that guesstimate balance is rarely close to the real amount. Make yourself write down every check, every deposit— every transaction—and the current balance at the moment it occurs. And don't forget transactions at the automatic- teller machines (ATMs) or with your debit or check card. Write them in your checking-account register at the time you make the withdrawal or purchase.
- *As much as possible, live with cash.* At times you will need to write checks; for example, when you send funds

through the mail. But in your day-to-day living, dealing with cash will revolutionize your financial life. When you leave the house in the morning and take only the amount of cash you'll need for the day, you won't be tempted to write checks for things you don't need or can't afford.

• *Stay away from slippery places.* Don't hang around the mall or pore over mail-order catalogs. And curtail your shopping on the Internet. Don't set yourself up for a fall if you are easily influenced to believe you need everything you see.

How to Begin Climbing out of the Hole

This entire book is about getting out of debt, learning to manage money responsibly, and gaining financial freedom. So you will find lots of ideas and strategies in the following chapters. For now, however, let's look at a few first steps that you can take to begin climbing out of the debt hole.

Commit to Honesty

When your financial life is all messed up, every area of your life is affected. Even your basic value system is vulnerable and open to attack. Few areas challenge your integrity as much as financial pressure. That's why such phrases as these have come into being: "The check's in the mail"; "I mailed it, so if it doesn't show up, I'll stop payment and send another"; and (to a department-store clerk), "There must be some mistake; I paid my account in full just last week!" Or maybe you've heard yourself or someone else say, "My check bounced? Oh, the bank screwed up my account. Just redeposit it." Need I go on?

As I mentioned in the last chapter, you must develop an attitude of honesty and integrity if you're going to get out of your mess and into the black. Make a pact between God and yourself that you are going to approach your finances with complete and brutal honesty. Let creditors with whom you've been less than honest in the past know that you are embarking on a financial-recovery plan.

Stop Debting

I understand that using the word *debt* (noun) as a verb *(to debt)* is rather unscholarly and grammatically incorrect. You won't find *debting* in the dictionary, but I like to use it because debting sounds wrong and *is* wrong. Debting has come to mean the act of owing money to another. To debt is the action of incurring a debt, as in *I debt, you debt, we debt* . . . you get the picture.

Debting can involve a personal loan from a parent or child; it can be unpaid rent or an installment purchase that does not involve collateral or one of who-knows-how-many other ways of getting something without paying for it now. These days, debting most commonly happens with a credit card. Consumer credit is rather plentiful, available in just about every retail store in the country. And the availability of that credit has plunged the vast majority of adult Americans into terrible debt. It has become the norm to spend what we do not have, and we are not the only ones to do it— look at our national debt. (I wouldn't dare quote a figure, for indeed it would be incorrect by the time this sentence is finished!)

Everywhere we turn, we're encouraged to buy what we want now, regardless of whether or not we have enough in cash or savings to pay for it, let alone whether or not we need it. We are encouraged to do it on credit—to buy now and pay (a lot more) later, including outrageous interest rates. Creditors often want to lull debtors into a false sense of security so that they will feel free to buy things that, on reflection, they would see they can't afford.

Compulsive debting is more than just an occasional meal charged on a bank card. It is the repeated use of credit, first by choice and later by necessity. In time, a big chunk of discretionary income is required to pay the minimum payments on the credit cards, and so, when an unexpected expense rears its ugly head, the debtor feels there is no choice but to incur yet another debt. Then the monthly payments are that much greater, causing that much more pressure. And so it goes. Eventually the credit sources will become "maxed out," but rarely in the case of a compulsive debtor will that stop the activity. A new way to debt will be found, and the problem will grow and grow.

There is only one way to reverse this process: *stop*. The best way to make sure you stop is to cut up the cards, cancel the accounts, and commit to the fastest payoff schedule possible. This is serious business, and stopping may very well be one of the hardest things you will ever do.

I'll not soon forget the day I was able to part with my cards. I felt stripped, naked, and violated. But one hour at a time, I was able to get hold of myself, and within a relatively short period, that empty, worthless feeling was replaced with one of freedom and relief as God filled my inadequacies with His power and strength.

Keep a Spending Record

We teach our children from a young age how to respect our privacy, and as they mature, their own rights to privacy are bestowed upon them. Little by little they become more self-governing and less accountable to outsiders until one day the fully matured, independent little birds are ready to leave the nest to make it on their own. Somewhere in that journey from the nest to the new nesting grounds, the transfer of accountability from parent to self should take place.

But in the area of finances, the process must have a high rate of breakdown because too many of us end up accountable to no one for our personal finances. And that aversion to accountability is our worst enemy. Here are a few examples: Have you any idea of the average amount you spent per month for food during the last year? How much do you spend on utilities in an average month? Auto repairs? Cab fare? What is the total amount of money you spent last month to service your debts? What percentage of that went toward debt reduction? What did you spend in coffee shops and on fast food . . . yesterday? Don't feel too bad—the typical person has a difficult time coming up with anything close to exact figures for such routine expenses.

I suppose denial has something to do with it. If you have no idea what your bank balance is, it is easy to play games and fool yourself by adding a digit or two instead of facing the possibility that you don't have enough in there to buy a newspaper, let alone cover the cash advance you managed to pull out of the ATM last night.

Assuming you are sick and tired of living in a financial fog, not knowing where all the money goes, then you desperately need the brilliant light that only a precise spending record will turn on in your life. You may be hesitant to bring into sharp focus the exact nature of your finances. And just as you must get used to a strong new pair of eyeglasses that correct fuzzy vision, you will have a period of adjustment with your spending record. You may even develop a headache. But you cannot overestimate the value and importance of recording your spending. Knowing the truth will set you free.

Here's how to get started: For the next thirty days, keep a Daily Spending Record. A spending record is simply a written accounting for money spent, including funds withdrawn from the ATM. And for now, keeping this record should not necessarily entail any changes in spending activity. You need to know how you spend your money, and this is the only way to find out. If you are part of a couple in which one person handles the bulk of the money, this will require a little teamwork. If you have an uncooperative partner, start by becoming accountable to yourself for whatever amount of money you control.

Get a notebook or pad of paper, something small and practical. Each day, start with a fresh page and put the current date at the top. Each time you spend cash or write a check, jot down two entries: what for and how much. That's it. One page per day, every day. No time off. No endless details and no totals (for now).

TYPICAL DAILY SPENDING RECORD

Date: _____

Tommy's lunch	$2.50
Coffee (2)	$1.89
Lunch	$3.78
Grocery store	$28.73
Rent	$850.00
Gasoline	$15.00
Jenny's school supplies	$5.80

At the end of the first week, gather up your seven individual records and merge them into one record, a Weekly Spending Record. I'm certain you'll be able to come up with a format that works perfectly for you, and it may not be exactly like mine. No matter how it looks, make sure that your record includes everything you've spent in the week, including checks you've written. Please don't make this more difficult than it is.

TYPICAL WEEKLY SPENDING RECORD

Week Number 1

Savings	$100.00
Groceries	$83.46
Food (away from home)	$52.73
Rent	$850.00
Telephone	$68.74
Gasoline	$30.00
Oil change/lube	$19.95
Clothing	$53.87
Kids' miscellaneous	$15.86
Gifts (Grandma's birthday)	$22.50
Household maintenance	$38.68
Magazines/subscriptions	$12.95
Newspapers	$1.75
Total Week Number 1	$1350.49

The next step is to convert four Weekly Spending Records into a Monthly Spending Record. The final step will be to develop your customized Monthly Spending Plan. But in order to do that, you will need the information coming up in chapters 7, 8, and 9.

Your assignment until we pick up this subject again in chapter 9 is to get comfortable with keeping Daily Spending Records and turning them into Weekly Spending Records every seven days.

Start Saving

Experts tell us that everyone should have cash put away to cover at least six months of expenses. When you are on the edge, that thought usually brings a sarcastic retort: "Yeah, right!" The goal line can seem a million miles away to someone starting on his own one-yard line. So start by having enough to cover one week, then move to a pay period and then to one month. At that point, you will at least have enough to live on until your unemployment checks kick in. Each time you make a savings deposit, you will be backing away from the edge, and that feels so good. (Chapter 6 will go into more detail on the best ways to start saving.)

Debt Keeps Us Living on the Edge

Whenever I think of the phrase *life on the edge,* I am propelled into childhood memories involving family automobile trips, great heights, and narrow roads. Without fail, I was always on the side of the car closest to the edge. And my front-row seat gave me a spectacular view of the bottomless canyon below with its giant mouth open, ready to swallow me up in the event I dared to come one inch closer. Add to that the perilous thought that I had absolutely no control over the situation, partly because I was a child but mostly because I couldn't reach the steering wheel or brake. One swerve, one jerk of the steering wheel and our car would have plummeted to disaster. I often thought how much more comfortable I would be if I were on the safe side of the car and my brother next to the edge—that way he would go first and break my fall.

Not until we were safe at last on the straight, flat, boring highway could I relax and enjoy the trip. How sad that I missed so much beauty while worrying about falling off the edge.

Like those fearful car trips along the brink of disaster, living on the edge of financial ruin is precarious and anxiety producing. Never having enough money to pay all of the bills, postdating a check or two, writing checks in hopes they won't clear until your next paycheck is deposited, committing next week's paycheck for this week's expenses, wondering how you would pay your bills if you lost your job tomorrow—all of these habits keep you living on the edge.

Living under this kind of gloominess can be depressing to say the least. The worst part is that so much energy is expended worrying and fretting that the beauty and joy of the moment are lost in the glare of stress and strain. But you don't have to live month after month feeling that if you come one inch closer, you will fall and be swallowed up by the jaws of financial ruin. Beginning with the simple steps we've discussed in this chapter and following the strategies outlined in the rest of this book will help you gain the peace of mind to enjoy the journey through life.

5

THE PRINCIPLE OF GIVING

Expose Yourself to

Supernatural Intervention

I hope you're not about to do what I fear you might—skip this chapter. I say that only because I know myself and I'm quite sure that's exactly what I would have done when my financial life was all messed up. Why waste time reading about what I already know I should do—and have such a hard time doing?

I grew up in church. I'm not exaggerating. As the daughter of a pastor in a medium-sized community, I spent many, many hours each week in some kind of church setting from nine months before my birth until I left home. I've heard a lot of sermons, many of which were on the subject of money and giving. As a kid, I knew this stuff so well I could have taught anyone about "giving back," or altruism. The problem is, the truth of that knowledge got stuck in my head. It didn't find its way into my heart until many years later.

I say this to assure you that what follows isn't from my head— it's from my heart. I get the same question over and over when people learn that I managed to run up an incredible six-figure amount of unsecured debt: "How did you ever pay it all back?!" My answer always startles the questioners, because, given the world's standards, it seems to be about the dumbest tactic one could think of. I reply, "We started giving away some of our money." Another way to put it is, we started following God's guidelines as found in the Bible. I don't know that I've ever felt such gratitude as I did in those early years of our financial recovery. I was so thankful to have money coming in at all that giving part of it to God was a pleasure.

A funny thing began to happen. More money came in. Opportunities arose for me to earn even more, which allowed us to start paying back the debts rapidly. As I look back, I am astounded by the ways God put the pieces of our financial puzzle back together. I couldn't really see it at the time, so it was pure trust that drove me to give.

I had the opportunity to enter the field of real estate at a time when it was a hot industry in southern California. I had no special education or experience to open those doors. I wasn't a member of a prestigious family with great wealth and standing in the community. And the oddest thing of all is that I am, obviously, a woman, and the industrial/commercial real-estate industry was—and continues to be—a male-dominated field. There was no reason, humanly speaking, that I should have ever been accepted, let alone found success, in that industry. I have no doubt that God blessed my heart's desire to change, pay back the debt, and obey Him in the area of giving.

You've probably heard it 1,000 times, but I'll make it 1,001: it's impossible to outgive God. I believe that with all my heart, because I have proven it over and over again.

Let's be careful here: I am not saying we should give in order to get. Some misguided teachers say that if we will just give enough, we will absolutely get tenfold in return from God. But that's nothing more than an attempt to manipulate God. Instead, we give to God first and foremost, including giving to help the needs of others, because that is what He's asked us to do. Having said that, I think everyone who makes a habit of giving would agree that blessings follow when we generously share our resources with others. The blessings might come in the form of joy and satisfaction, or as new opportunities.

The act of giving is itself fabulous, but it has many side benefits as well:

- *Giving to God is an act of worship.* By offering to God the best of what we have with hearts full of love and gratitude, we are worshiping the One who provides for all our needs. We acknowledge that God is the creator of all and that our very existence depends on him.

- *Giving to God is an act of trust.* I can't say I actually understand how this works—how it is that in giving we receive—but I have seen it in operation time after time. Giving out of your abundance is an act of thanksgiving, but giving out of your need is an act of faith.

- *Giving to God promotes humility.* By sharing our money with others—rather than hoarding it and holding it with clenched fists—we acknowledge that what we have really belongs to God, not to us. We are entrusted with resources and charged with the responsibility to use them to help others. Nothing will quiet our greed and cure a case of the "I-wants" like giving away part of our income.

- *Giving to God helps us find balance.* The perfect formula for creating balance in your finances is to give away 10 percent, save 10 percent, and then learn to live within the 80 percent that's left. I love the way those figures fit together—it's all so tidy and orderly. While this is a wonderful formula, let me say that there's nothing magical about giving 10 percent. That is, I believe we should give as we've been given. So as you attain greater and greater financial freedom, you may choose to pass along more and more of your money to those in need.

• *Giving to God is a demonstration of gratitude.* We give to God because we love Him and are grateful for all that He has done for us. Giving from a thankful heart while expecting nothing in return is a sweet offering to the One who owns everything anyway. It's the least we can do.

How much of our income to give away and whom should we give it to are personal decisions that each of us must make in accordance with our faith. Nevertheless, let me suggest some guidelines to help you through the decision-making process:

1. Give first. If you deposit your income into the bank, then go about your weekly activities with the intention of giving later, you probably won't. I suggest that you make up some payment coupons similar to those you have for your mortgage payment. Put them at the front of your bills-to-be-paid folder to ensure that making that payment is the first thing you do. Giving will become a habit provided you repeat the act over and over.

2. Give wisely. I suggest that if you are part of a church, you should support that ministry financially because that is where you are receiving spiritually. When considering other ministries or charitable organizations, first request a current financial report. Learn what they are doing, how they do it, and who is in charge. I am suspicious of any organization that is not open with its financial affairs and any whose overhead and administrative costs exceed 25 percent. In other words, at least 75¢ of every dollar I give should make it to the actual work I wish to support.

3. *Give quietly.* Don't trumpet the fact that you give money away. Give because it is the right thing to do and because you are grateful for all that's been given to you— not because you want other people to admire your generosity and benevolence.

4. *Give joyfully.* You may not feel all that obedient or grateful when you begin to follow this principle of giving. That's okay. Ask God to make your heart joyful, and just keep giving. The feelings of joy will come. It's much easier to act your way into a feeling than to feel your way into an action.

When you are worried, filled with anxiety, or just feeling greedy, give! It is the best all-purpose remedy I know for money troubles. The following account by Dr. Norman Vincent Peale is a wonderful illustration of the blessings that come from giving.*

Back in 1930, I was a young married minister in Syracuse, New York. My salary, which had been a handsome (in those days) $6,000 a year, was cut twice—first to $5,000, then to $4,000. We had no manse or home supplied by the church. Everyone was frightened and depressed. Businesses were failing. Nobody could borrow money; there was no money to be had. Men used to greet one another grimly by saying, "Have you had your pay cut yet?" Everyone had to take several cuts

---

*Quoted by permission of *Plus* magazine, vol. 40, no. 4 (Part III), May 1989. Copyright © 1989 Foundation for Christian Living, Pawling, N.Y.

before that depression ended, and many people lost their jobs altogether.

With a salary of $4,000 a year, I just didn't see how we could get by. My salary was the only income we had. I was helping my younger brother with college expenses, and I knew he had to count on that. The pressure got worse and worse. I hated to burden Ruth [Peale's wife] with my fears. One night I went out alone and walked through Walnut Park near our little apartment, and for the first time in my life I felt icy terror clutching at my mind and heart. I was terrified. When I finally went home, I said to Ruth, "We're in a desperate situation. We can't pay the bills. What are we going to do?"

And her answer really startled me. She said, "We're going to start tithing."

"Tithing?" I echoed. "We can't! It's impossible!"

"Not impossible," Ruth said. "Essential. You know what the Old Testament promises to those who give 10 percent of everything to the Lord." I can see her yet, standing in the kitchen and quoting, "Bring ye all the tithes into the store-house . . . and prove Me now herewith, said the Lord of hosts, if I will not open you the windows of heaven and pour you out a blessing that there shall not be room enough to receive it" (Mal. 3:10).

"We're going to do that," she said stoutly, "because tithing is an act of faith and the Bible says that if we have faith even as small as a grain of mustard seed, nothing will be impossible for us. We have to start imagining God's prosperity."

So we did it. And Ruth was right. Money didn't pour in, but there always was enough. Furthermore, the act of tithing calmed my fears and stimulated my mind so that I began thinking. I started imagining. I knew I had one small talent: public speaking. And so I offered myself as a public speaker *wherever one was needed. I spoke at civic clubs and garden clubs and graduations and community gatherings. Sometimes I was paid five or 10 dollars, sometimes nothing at all. But it helped. What a thrill I felt when I received the first $25 fee. Then someone who heard me speak offered me a chance to go on radio. Again, I received no money for this, but the number of speaking invitations increased. So one thing led to another and gradually we began to get our heads above water.*

I am convinced that tithing did it. Ruth and I have been tithers ever since. Through the years in sermons and talks I have recommended tithing to thousands of people and hundreds have been persuaded to try it. Of those hundreds, not one has ever told me that the experiment failed, that he regretted it, or that it was a mistake. Not a single person.

It's almost as if there is an invisible reservoir of abundance in the universe that can be tapped if you will just obey certain spiritual laws. The word abundance, I'm told, comes from a Latin phrase meaning to "rise up in waves." When you tithe, it does seem as if little waves of abundance start rising up all around you.

So if you have financial difficulties, face up to them not just with courage and intelligence, but also with warmhearted generosity and concern for others.

6

The Principle of Saving

Part of Everything You Earn
Is Yours to Keep

The edge is a miserable place to live. People who exist from paycheck to paycheck live there. They spend all they have. And when something unexpected happens, the choice is to either take a flying leap into the darkness below or run to the credit cards, the finance company, or worse, the bankruptcy court.

The antidote to living on the edge is simple: *Move away!* It starts with a single step away from the edge. And then another and another until you have created enough space between where you live and the edge that you can relax—and sleep at night.

That space is called a Contingency Fund. It is a tangible hedge of protection. This fund is a pool of money that you can get your hands on in a short period of time and that is stored in a safe place that pays at least enough interest to stay ahead of inflation. Creating and maintaining your Contingency Fund are an important part of your plan to debt-proof your life.

A Contingency Fund has nothing to do with your investments.

It is also not the money in the Freedom Account that you build up over the months to pay your unexpected, irregular, and intermittent expenses. (We will discuss the details of the Freedom Account in chapter 8.) A Contingency Fund is not for discretionary spending but rather is a pool of money set aside for major catastrophes so that you do not have to run for credit. This fund will be available if you lose your job, or when your safety or health is at risk.

Financial experts suggest a typical family needs the equivalent of three to six months of living expenses in reserve. I find that suggestion too nebulous and prefer to take the advice of my colleague, Austin Pryor, author of *Sound Mind Investing*, who suggests a fund of $10,000. That amount seems about right for the average family. If your monthly expenses are high, however, you should adjust that to the amount you would need to live for a full three months without any income.

When to Use the Fund

Think of your Contingency Fund as your personal debt insurance. Its short-term purpose is to provide an alternative to using credit to cover emergencies for which you are not otherwise prepared, such as auto repairs and medical bills. Eventually your Contingency Fund will become your second line of defense against debt, with this primary purpose: to be the bridge you will need in the event you and your income temporarily part company. It is difficult enough to get out of debt, but if you are continually adding new debt because of such emergencies, it becomes nearly impossible.

The 10 percent of your income I suggest you pay to yourself— save—should be parked in your Contingency Fund. If you currently have a savings account, you can designate that as your

Contingency Fund and then begin adding to it on a regular basis. The goal is to accumulate and then maintain, as your normal way of life, a $10,000 Contingency Fund, or enough to pay all of your expenses for three months (six is better) without any income, whichever is greater. If you find it necessary to withdraw money from your fund, your top savings priority should be replacing that money as soon as possible until the fund is restored to the full $10,000.

Where to Park It

You will be tempted to start seeing your Contingency Fund as a long-term investment. Avoid doing that, because this isn't an investment; it is money to be available to you in an emergency. Such insurance will keep you afloat if your income temporarily stops. In looking for a place to park your Contingency Fund, you need to be concerned about safety, availability, and growth, in that order.

SAFETY. It must be in an account where the principal is not at risk. This is why your Contingency Fund should not be invested in the stock market.

AVAILABILITY. Because of the nature of emergencies, this fund needs to be liquid, meaning that you could get your hands on at least part of it within twenty-four to forty-eight hours.

GROWTH. You will maintain your Contingency Fund for many years. As a good steward, you want to expose your resources to the best compounding interest available that still meets the safety and availability requirements.

Getting Started

Whether you have no savings now or have a great start on accumulating at least $10,000, you'll want to start thinking about where to put it.

If you have no savings now, you should open an account at your credit union or bank with your first deposit. The type of account will depend on the amount of money you have available to get started.

Credit Unions Versus Banks

Banks are for-profit corporations, while credit unions are nonprofit organizations existing for the benefit of their members. When a credit union generates a surplus, it is paid out to account holders in the form of either a small dividend or a rebate of loan interest at the end of the fiscal year. Typically, credit-union fees are lower than those at banks, while their interest rates are a bit higher. If you are eligible to join a credit union, consider it an excellent place to park your Contingency Fund and to let it grow. Deposits in banks are federally insured up to $100,000. Deposits in *most* credit unions are also federally insured, a feature you definitely want.

Credit Union and Bank Accounts

When you walk into a bank or credit union to open an account for your Contingency Fund, you'll be given a choice that may include the following:

- *Passbook savings account.* This is at the bottom of the savings ladder but a good place for newbies. You can expect low interest and low minimum requirements.

- *NOW account.* Even though this is an interest-bearing checking account, you might consider it in the beginning. Just make sure any checks the bank issues you are put away in an inconvenient, yet safe, place. You don't want to slip and think this is a checking account from which you can start making withdrawals. You will find the interest rate a bit higher than that of the passbook savings account, but expect a minimum requirement of $1,500.

- *SuperNOW account.* This is similar to the NOW Account, with better interest and a higher minimum requirement of $2,000 to $2,500. Ditto with that checkbook.

- *Bank money-market accounts.* Do not confuse this with money-market funds offered by *mutual-fund companies.* While bank money-market accounts carry the same federal insurance provision as other bank deposits, they typically pay lower interest than a money-market fund from a mutual-fund company.

- *Certificates of deposit.* CDs are similar to passbook savings accounts in that you deposit the money and are paid a set rate of interest. The difference is that, in exchange for your promise to leave the money for a set period of time (90 days, 180 days, 1 year, etc.), you are guaranteed a higher rate of interest. If you must withdraw early, a penalty will apply to the interest portion only. The penalty will never touch your principal. Shorter-term CDs yield slightly less interest.

Nonbank Considerations

U.S. TREASURIES. You can lend your money to the U.S. government in the form of treasury bills (short-term government bonds). If this sounds like a place you'd like to park your Contingency Fund, you need to do a little homework. First, get a copy of

Buying Treasury Securities. Call the Federal Reserve branch closest to you to request a copy plus a complete packet of forms and information available for first-time investors. If you cannot find a local branch, call the federal branch in Los Angeles, 213-624-7398. You can open an account and make your purchases by phone, 800-943-6864, or online at http://www.publicdebt.treas.gov/sec/sectrdir.htm. The minimum investment required for treasury bills is $1,000. Government securities are sold at auction, and you will need to learn the process in order to become an active participant.

MONEY-MARKET FUND ACCOUNTS. These are different from money-market accounts at a bank. A money-market fund is a large pool of money managed by professionals and invested in safe and stable securities, including commercial paper (short-term IOUs of large U.S. corporations), treasury bills, and large bank CDs. Money-market funds are a very attractive place to grow a Contingency Fund because:

1. *Safety.* Even though not guaranteed by the federal government, this type of account is regulated by the Securities and Exchange Commission.

2. *Liquidity.* Deposits are not tied to any time frames, which means your funds are available at any time and in any amount. You can take out only the amount you need.

3. *Higher rates of interest.* The return on money-market fund accounts is typically 1 to 1.5 percentage points higher than the return on bank or credit-union accounts.

4. *Check-writing privileges.* This feature allows you to have access to the funds without going through phone calls and wire transfers. You cannot think of this as a checking account, and that's good. Money-market fund accounts have

restrictions against writing checks for small amounts, say, less than $200. Typically no fees are imposed or restrictions made on the number of checks that can be written in a month.

If your funds are parked in a money-market fund, you don't have to worry about maturity dates, the possibility of early-withdrawal penalties, or getting in before the auction closes. The interest-effective yield (interest rate) moves with the general state of the economy.

While most money-market fund accounts require a minimum deposit of at least $2,500, some waive that requirement if you have authorized automatic deposits of at least $50 a month.

Literally hundreds of money-market funds are available from which to choose if you decide this is a good place for your Contingency Fund. Before opening any account, call for and read a prospectus so that you fully understand the rules and risks involved. With the prospectus you will receive an application that looks daunting but is actually quite simple to complete. If you have any questions, you can call the toll-free customer-service number.

I recommend that you consider a money-market fund account for your Contingency Fund and that you also sign up for automatic deposit authorization. Now you will have the best of all worlds with the least amount of baby-sitting.

REPUTABLE MONEY-MARKET FUNDS		
Fund Name	*Minimum to Open*	*Telephone*
American Century Prime Money Market	$2,500	800-472-3389
Vanguard Prime Portfolio	$3,000	800-662-7447
USAA Money Market	$3,000*	800-531-8181
Strong Money Market Fund	$2,500	800-368-3863

*Exception: The minimum deposit is waived if you authorize automatic monthly deposits of at least $50.

Figure 6.1

Automatic-Deposit Authorization

I am a *huge* proponent of automatic deposits, especially when it comes to building a savings or investment account. With my busy lifestyle and my tendency to put things off, I know I would forget or find some reason to skip my savings deposits from time to time. I can simplify my life by authorizing my bank or investment-account manager to reach into my checking account on a specified day every month to take out the amount I authorize. In a way it's like delegating work to someone else so I can be free to do what I do best. I think of it as hiring a staff person to handle the savings and deposits I'm committed to.

If you have any tendencies toward procrastination and feel

better when things are taken care of for you, I suggest you think seriously about arranging for automatic deposits into your Contingency Fund. In the beginning you might feel the pinch of having your savings automatically deducted from your regular checking account and deposited into your savings vehicle. But before you know it, you will become accustomed to the lower amount. What you don't see, you won't miss, and you won't have to worry about remembering to make that transfer of funds. Some larger employers offer payroll-deduction plans. You simply fill out an authorization form with the specific information on your account numbers. Then your pay stubs will indicate that the money has been deposited automatically. Of course, you can change your automatic-deposit authorization anytime. You can increase the amount, change the date, or even change your mind. You're the boss.

Just as giving is a key to your Money Makeover, your Contingency Fund is foundational to changing your financial future. Make the commitment to reaching that $10,000 goal. Shop around for the best places to park your money (see Figures 6.2 and 6.3 for timetables on reaching your goal at different interest rates). Once you have a fund and your automatic deposits in place, you're on the way to controlling your money instead of letting it control you.

NUMBER OF MONTHS REQUIRED TO ACCUMULATE $10,000 4% ANNUAL INTEREST					
If you start with	*Assuming you add this much each month*				
	$100	$150	$200	$250	$300
$0	87	61	47	38	32
$500	82	57	44	36	30
$1000	77	54	42	34	29
$2000	67	48	37	30	25
$3000	58	41	32	26	22
$5000	41	29	23	19	16

Figure 6.2

NUMBER OF MONTHS REQUIRED TO ACCUMULATE $10,000 6% ANNUAL INTEREST					
If you start with	*Assuming you add this much each month*				
	$100	$150	$200	$250	$300
$0	81	58	45	37	31
$500	77	55	43	35	30
$1000	72	51	40	33	28
$2000	62	45	35	29	25
$3000	54	39	31	25	22
$5000	37	27	22	18	15

Figure 6.3

7

The Principle
of Living Debt-Free

*How to Develop Your Rapid
Debt-Repayment Plan*

Several years ago I received the following letter, and it is still one of the most memorable letters ever sent to me.

Like a lot of people, I got my first credit card with a feeling of "having arrived," and I declared it "only for emergencies." I still remember a coworker's laugh when I said that. Five years later I had six cards, all maxed out due to "emergencies," and then I understood what prompted her chuckle. I owe for car repairs on a car I no longer own, furniture that I sold in a garage sale, braces that came off my son's teeth a year ago. But worst of all, my balances include several thousand dollars' worth of expenses I don't even remember.

Everyone who goes into debt and successfully digs out has a turning point. Mine came when Christmas arrived and I found myself buried in bills with no more room to charge on any cards. I took a job working for minimum wage at a department store for the holidays. My entire Christmas season was miserable because I was exhausted and had no time to enjoy festivities with my family. But it was such a valuable experience that I recommend this to anyone sinking into credit-card hell.

Working in that store, I saw credit from a whole different perspective. Customers would make a small payment on a huge balance, charge twice that while they were in the store, and pay several times as much in the end on already overpriced merchandise because they had their credit line and no cash reserves. They bought top-of-the-line clothing and housewares to give as gifts in order to keep up appearances but confessed they would never be able to afford these things for themselves. As a cashier, I knew before they got to the register which customers would charge their purchases; they were the ones with the tired, sad expressions, the ones who were obviously not enjoying the holiday season or anything else. I felt guilty suggesting purchases and putting their selections on account, because I was helping make their lives worse. (The training staff at this store instructed us to suggest the highest-priced options and to sell by pushing low payments while never divulging the number of payments.) I even felt bad giving discounts to entice first-time credit-card buyers because I knew the merchandise they were buying would not last as long as the payments. The giddy look on newlyweds' faces when they first discovered they had more buying power than cash looked sickeningly familiar. That's the bad news.

The good news is, for the first time in years I made up my mind to get off that merry-go-round forever. I am now going in the opposite direction—out of the hole instead of deeper in. Since the beginning of the year, I have devised and stuck with a two-year financial-recovery plan, and I'm beginning to see real results.

Ironically, I am beginning to feel the same things I felt years ago when I got my first credit card: powerful, in charge, secure, and prepared for emergencies. Only this time, the emotions are based in reality. Thank you again for your wonderful publications.

—McKenzey

If you want to sabotage your Money Makeover, keep on incurring new debts. That's right. Just keep those credit cards charged right up to the max, and as your income increases over the years, make sure you get into as much debt as possible. That way, no matter how much you work at reducing your expenses and saving for the future, your debts will stick with you right to the grave, weighing you down and robbing you of happiness. You can make sure you are just one more person who only *dreamed* of enjoying wonderful things and seeing beautiful places because you never quite got your money straightened out.

On the other hand, if you are excited about the possibility of changing the way you deal with money, developing new money attitudes, and experiencing happiness and satisfaction from knowing how to handle your resources in an intelligent and reasoned way, then it is mandatory that you stop incurring debt and reverse that destructive behavior. Designing your own Rapid Debt-Repayment Plan is an important part of your Money Makeover.

Reality Check

Allow me to introduce you to a rarely thought of and even more rarely enjoyable activity called *debt repayment*. This may come as a shock, but your debts have to be repaid somehow, somewhere, sometime. The credit-card companies are not in business to supply you with free clothes and fancy meals. That was a big shock to me, too—a terrible reality I had to face. If you are relying on the minimum monthly payments to pay off your debt anytime soon, think again.

Let's say you owe $2,000 on your credit card, which charges 19.8 percent interest for the privilege. Your minimum monthly payment is 3 percent of the outstanding balance, which is presently $60 and fluctuates each month depending on the principal. All that's required is $60, so that's all you pay, right? If you make only the minimum payment each month, how long do you think it will take you to pay off that $2,000 if you never make another purchase? I'll tell you: 19 years and 4 months, assuming your payments are never late and you do not add any new purchases. By the time you finish, you will have paid interest in the amount of $4,318.12. That's $2,000—plus $4,318.12!

If you are a typical consumer—i.e., a preferred and valued customer, meaning you keep your credit cards "maxed out" or at least make sure there's a good, healthy balance rolling over from month to month—it is highly unlikely your consumer debt will ever be paid off. You will continue to pay this month for food you consumed years ago, clothes you've long since given away, and other stuff you've undoubtedly forgotten about completely. That, my friends, is perma-debt, and the credit-card companies love it.

Let's go back to the example of the $2,000 debt, which requires a monthly minimum payment of $60. What if, through some stroke of unexplained sense, you made a solemn and personal pledge to pay $60 every month until the darned thing was paid in full, choosing to ignore that the actual monthly minimum payment requirement was going down every month? You would reach a zero balance in just 49 months, instead of 232 months (19 years, 4 months). And if you got really sane and committed to paying $90 a month? The debt would be history in just 28 months. Brace yourself here. Let's assume you *really* lost your mind and made a personal pledge to pay $100 a month against the $2,000 debt. You would pay it off in just 24 months, more than 17 years sooner than if you believed the credit-card company when it said all you have to pay is the minimum monthly balance. I never cease to be amazed at the power of compounded interest and what it can do to your financial picture.

Plan Your Work and Work Your Plan

All of us who are intimately familiar with overspending know that it is very easy to five-and-ten-dollar ourselves into oblivion. The good news is that you can five-and-ten-dollar yourself right back to financial health, too. The key to rapid debt repayment is to make a plan and stick to it as if your life depended on it. It may. The details of the plan you devise for your own debt reduction are not nearly as important as your determination to carry it out.

Several methods of rapid debt reduction work equally well. One method involves a plan whereby each of your debts is paid off proportionately so that they all reach zero balance at the same time.

However, the method I will teach you (which is, coincidentally, my personal favorite) is based on the principle that it feels good to work extra hard on one bill at a time in order to experience the exhilaration of a zero balance as quickly as possible. Paying off one debt completely gives a great boost to your determination to pay off the next and the next and the next.

While it does not provide instant gratification, this method certainly offers short-term achievable goals. Small doses of gratification along the way keep you motivated. Here's how it works:

The first thing you must do is determine exactly how much you owe and the exact nature of your debts. We are talking about unsecured debt—anything that you owe that would not be subject to repossession if you stopped paying—such as credit-card balances, personal loans, or payments you are making to the dentist or doctor. Make a list of all of the unsecured debts, outlining the current balance, minimum payment, interest rate, and number of payments required to pay the amount in full. If you do not possess the math skills required to figure out how many payments will be required to pay off the debt, use a financial calculator or call each creditor and ask. With their super computer programs, they should be able to tell you. (However, they may be reluctant to.) *Cheapskate Monthly* offers a number of financial calculators, including the Rapid Debt-Repayment Plan calculator, as a part of its online membership. For more information, or to check out the Rapid Debt-Repayment Plan calculator demonstration, visit www. cheapskatemonthly.com.

Next, arrange these debts in order of the number of months required to pay each in full, with the shortest payoff first on the list. (See the "Sam and Samantha Example" chart on page 69. The debt they placed first on the list has a balance of $80. With a minimum payment of $35, it will take just a bit longer than two months to pay it off, which is less than any of their other debts will require.)

Next, add up the total of the current minimum monthly payments. This is an important number, so write it down, embed it in your brain, tattoo it on your forehead, paint it on your walls, teach it to your children. This number for the Examples is $619 each month.

SAM AND SAMANTHA EXAMPLE'S RAPID DEBT-REPAYMENT PLAN
Debt-free in just 24 months

Creditor	$ Bal	%	1	2	3	4	5	6	7	8	9	10	11	12	13	14	15	16	17	18	19	20	21	22	23	24
Dept. Store #1	80	16.9	35	35	12	0																					
Personal Loan	700	10	108	108	131	143	89	0																		
Student Loan	200	6	26	26	26	26	80	163	0																	
Visa #1	1,500	18	108	108	108	108	108	114	277	277	277	277	209	0												
Orthodontist	1,000	18	40	40	40	40	40	40	40	40	40	40	108	317	317	0										
Credit Union	3,000	12	120	120	120	120	120	120	120	120	120	120	120	120	120	437	437	437	437	437	145	0				
Finance Co.	1,200	14	45	45	45	45	45	45	45	45	45	45	45	45	45	45	45	45	45	45	337	278	0			
MasterCard	1,000	19.6	40	40	40	40	40	40	40	40	40	40	40	40	40	40	40	40	40	40	40	244	264	0		
Visa #2	650	18	32	32	32	32	32	32	32	32	32	32	32	32	32	32	32	32	32	32	32	32	128	0		
Dept. Store #2	2,000	18.5	65	65	65	65	65	65	65	65	65	65	65	65	65	65	65	65	65	65	65	65	227	619	519	0
Totals	11,330		619	619	619	619	619	619	619	619	619	619	619	619	619	619	619	619	619	619	619	619	619	619	519	

Debt Free!

Figure 7.1

And now . . . it's commitment time. Look again at the total of your minimum monthly payments—the number you've just embedded in your brain. This is the amount of money you must commit to paying toward your Rapid Debt-Repayment Plan until all of your debts are paid. I don't think you should find this at all out of line, because this is the amount you have to pay every month anyway (assuming you don't skip payments). At this time I am not asking you to pay any more than you are required to pay. (It wouldn't be such a bad idea, but it's not required.) This is the minimum amount you must devote to your Rapid Debt-Repayment Plan regardless of whether or not this is the minimum amount according to your creditors. Remember, they want you to pay less every month so you can keep paying forever.

Here is what happens next: You continue to pay the same amount each month, even as your debts go down. When you pay off one debt, you don't reduce the amount you're paying toward debt reduction—you apply what you were paying on the first debt to the next debt, and so on, until all the debts are paid off.

Look at the Examples' Rapid Debt-Repayment Plan. This is how it works: The total of minimum monthly payments in the first month is $619. This is the amount Sam and Samantha have committed to paying every month until they are debt-free, regardless of anything their creditors say about lower payments. In month 1, the Examples make all of the minimum monthly payments for a total of $619. In month 2, they do the same thing. In month 3, they make their committed payments just as they did in the past two months—except now the payment to Department Store number 1 is only $12 because that is the total outstanding balance. Wow! The first zero balance. So what happens to the $23 they don't have to send to Department Store number 1 because of the zero balance? That $23 is included with the regular payment to Personal Loan (the next debt in line), increasing its payment from $108 to $131.

In month 4, the $35 payment that used to go to Department Store number 1 is now added to Personal Loan's payment, so that it becomes $143. This additional payment (technically prepayment of the principal) is what will get that Personal Loan paid in just six months, including interest. The total amount paid in month 4 is still $619 even though the number of debts has been reduced.

Now look at what happened to the Student Loan while this was going on. It reached a zero balance in month 7 as well, so now Sam and Samantha have three debts completely paid off. But since they are committed to paying $619 every month against their debts, the payment to Visa number 1 is substantially increased because the old payments for Department Store number 1, Personal Loan, and Student Loan are all added to the Visa number 1 payment, increasing it from $108 to $277 until it is fully paid in month 11.

And on it goes. The Examples pay $619 every month, always taking the old payments and adding them to the payment of the next debt until month 23, when they are 100 percent debt-free!

You must agree that this is truly amazing, considering that with the slow-pay method Sam and Samantha would have been paying these debts for twelve or more years, provided that they never missed a payment and did not incur any new debt.

Let's Review

Here are the five steps for wiping out your debts in record time:

STEP 1: *You must repent. Repent* simply means to turn around, to go in a different direction. You must turn around from debting; that is, from incurring new debts. If you don't complete this first step, the plan will not work.

STEP 2: *You must pay the same amount every month until all of your unsecured debts are paid in full.* From this moment on, you must adopt the total of your current minimum monthly payments as your regular monthly obligation, not unlike your house or car payment. It will not change from month to month. It's big, it's ugly, and it's not going to disappear. Just accept it.

STEP 3: *List your debts in order according to the number of months left.* For example, a debt to a department store of $80 total with a minimum monthly payment of $40 has about 2 months left (the total paid will be slightly higher than the $80 because of the interest). That one goes at the top of your list. Then, if the next debt will take 5 months to pay off, that's listed next; then the 9-month debt, and so on.

STEP 4: *From here on out, ignore declining minimum monthly payments.* The minimum payment in the first month of your plan is the amount you will pay until your total debt is wiped out, regardless of whether the creditor shows a lower amount due on your statement. Don't succumb to the temptation to reduce your payments as your debts are reduced.

STEP 5: *As one debt is paid off, apply its monthly payment to the next debt.* No matter how many debts you have paid off, you must commit to paying the same total amount every month until every debt is paid.

If you want to see your Rapid Debt-Repayment Plan work even more quickly, increase your monthly commitment. Remember that the key to rapid repayment is in prepaying the principal.

Take hope from these two letters from people who benefited from the Rapid Debt-Reduction Plan:

I just want to say thank you—you've really opened my eyes. My Rapid Debt-Repayment Plan has me completely paid off in 36 months.

I owed $14,000 in credit-card debt. You're right, you get into a set pace of living the good life without realizing what you are doing to your future. In one month, I charged $1,428 in clothing on my Visa card without a second thought (at 21 percent interest!).

I got into the habit of living well when I married a man who made an incredible salary; when we divorced, it was nearly impossible to cut back. I tried to maintain the lifestyle to which I'd become accustomed. I've had to face reality, and it's been tough.

I'll be completely debt-free when I'm thirty-four years old, and I can't wait!

—Mary Beth

I want to let you know that I am completely debt-free! I've carried some amount of debt since I got my first credit card nearly fifteen years ago. Paying the monthly bills was just a fact of life. But I followed your Rapid Debt-Repayment Plan and paid off my debts in three years. I discovered that debt doesn't have to be a way of life. I didn't realize the burden I was carrying until the last credit-card payment was mailed off. I feel free!

I shudder to think how much money I paid in interest—in fact, it would probably make me ill to calculate how big my savings would be right now if I had all the interest money back. So I'll focus on the positive: no debt . . . and no debt ever again.

—Jerry

8

THE PRINCIPLE OF PREPARATION

How to Develop Your Freedom Account

We are about to uncover what I am sure is a major source of your financial difficulties. I have read so many letters and talked to so many people about their financial situations that I have begun to see a pattern. To my utter amazement, the majority of these people are simply repeating what happened to me.

Most people learn to fit their regular monthly expenses into their average monthly income. In other words, there's no cushion, no fudge room. It may not be an exemplary way to handle personal finances, but it's the way most people get by. Somehow the rent gets paid, food arrives on the table, the car payment is met, and the utility companies keep providing electricity, water, and gas.

Since monthly income covers these predictable monthly payments, it is easy to get comfortable, to feel that everything is just peachy. So peachy, in fact, that it seems okay to take on a little extra debt ("It's only $15 a month, dear!") or make purchases with discretionary income (which we mistakenly define as anything that represents a balance in the checkbook). It's all right to have a few extra dinners out because there are a few extra bucks in the checking account. It's fine to splurge here and there because we seem to have enough money.

Without our noticing, monthly income and regular monthly expenses have a way of becoming dangerously close. What little cushion might have existed is eaten away by the extras. Occasional pay increases provide breathing room for a short time, but they are quickly absorbed into thin air, or so it seems.

The problem is something I call selective amnesia—a form of denial found far too often among those who can least afford such a malady. Let's look at the symptoms of selective amnesia and their debilitating consequences. One symptom, for instance, is being totally unaware that the car is wearing out with every mile driven. We don't come right out and say it, but we live as though somehow our tires are the only ones on planet Earth made of indestructible material. Each month that we do not experience flat tires or blowouts just confirms this mysterious supposition. Since the car starts up every morning, doesn't leak oil, and shifts gears flawlessly month after month, we live as if it will always perform at its current level of excellence. When it comes to any kind of automobile maintenance beyond the ceremonial oil change, most people slip easily into selective amnesia.

What's more, this condition applies to far more than automobiles. Most people think their house will never need repairs, their refrigerator will never die, their hard drive will never crash, and their clothes will never wear out.

Meet the Freedom Account

Somehow you manage to pay your rent or mortgage every month because past experience has taught you that failure to do so brings swift and painful consequences. Imagine you are notified that, effective immediately, you will no longer pay rent (or the mortgage payment) monthly but rather in one lump sum for the entire year. Your first yearly payment will be due one year from today.

Since you aren't required to pay the rent each month, would 1/12 of that annual payment be as critical to you on a monthly basis as it is now? Probably not. More than likely, rent would become one of your annual expenses that you hope will somehow take care of itself when the time comes. Knowing yourself, what do you think your chances are of coming up with the, oh, let's say $12,000 annual payment one year from now? About as good as the chances that you put away cash for most of your other intermittent expenses! It would be natural (though not too smart) for you to feel some relief in knowing you will no longer have to deal with rent on a monthly basis. Some of us would actually experience a feeling of exhilaration in calculating how this new arrangement will free up an "extra" $1,000 each month. Others (those who are breaking out in a cold sweat at this very moment) know the only right way to respond is to act as if 1/12 of the rent is still "due" every month and put that amount under the mattress or in a coffee can religiously on the first day of each month, no matter what. Wise people would live no differently than if the rent were due every month.

Lest any of you get too used to such an insane idea, let me bring you back to reality. Your rent or mortgage payment is due every month just as it always has been. And 1/12 of your automobile maintenance is due every month along with 1/12 of your property taxes and 1/12 of quite a few things that you fail to consider on a monthly basis. Expenses that are not paid monthly are called *irregular expenses.* This is where selective amnesia becomes a virtual epidemic. When it comes to irregular expenses, many people become amnesiacs.

Talk is cheap, isn't it? And at no time is it cheaper than when you have to say you're going to start planning ahead for the irregular expenses. However, I will teach you a method that, if followed diligently, will change your life forever. This is so exciting, so effective, so easy to handle, it borders on being miraculous. It's called (drumroll, please) the Freedom Account, and it is truly the key to turning your financial life around forever.

Developing a Freedom Account

The key to achieving financial ease is exerting control over your money. You can bring order and purpose to your personal finances by regularly setting aside funds in advance to cover your irregular expenses. Opening a Freedom Account will bring you a new sense of dignity, control, and personal worth. Here's how:

STEP 1: *Determine irregular expenses.* Using last year's check registers or paid-bills folder, make a list of expenses that you do not pay on a regular monthly basis. These expenses might be paid quarterly, semiannually, or annually. Multiply to reach an annual figure and then divide by twelve so you can arrive at a figure that represents 1/12 of the total annual expense.

Here are some expenses Sam and Samantha Example, our fictitious sample family of four, calculated to be their irregular expenses. Please don't get hung up on these dollar figures and miss the principles they represent. They are fabricated and do not necessarily indicate what is typical.

Auto Maintenance/Repairs	$ 900/yr. divided by 12 = $75/mo.
Auto Insurance	$ 720/yr. divided by 12 = $60/mo.
Life Insurance	$ 480/yr. divided by 12 = $40/mo.
Property Taxes	$ 600/yr. divided by 12 = $50/mo.
Vacation	$1200/yr. divided by 12 = $100/mo.
Clothing	$ 600/yr. divided by 12 = $50/mo.
	Total: $375/mo.

Sam and Samantha receive their income monthly; therefore, they will handle their Freedom Account on a monthly basis. You may not be paid once a month; however, since it would be impossible for me to convert every illustration to fit your particular payroll schedule, I'll leave it to you to translate the principles herein to fit your particular circumstances.

STEP 2: *Open two checking accounts.* Yes, two. Shop for a bank or credit union that offers the best terms available, such as no fee with a minimum balance, low-fee, or interest-bearing checking accounts with minimum balance. Open the two accounts at the same time and order checks for each account. (I highly recommend duplicate checks even though they cost a bit more.) Have them personalized and add the words *Regular Account* and *Freedom Account* under your name and address on the accounts and checks. If you wish to continue using your present checking account for the regular account, simply open a second at the same institution. The point is that you need to have two active checking accounts at a bank that will offer you the best terms and services. Do not—I repeat, do not—accept an ATM card for the Freedom Account. Having ATM access to this account will defeat its purpose.

The regular account will continue to accommodate your monthly expenses and typical day-to-day needs, such as groceries, gas, etc. You will continue to deposit your regular paychecks and other forms of income into this account.

STEP 3: *Request an automatic-deposit authorization.* At the time you open the accounts, request an automatic-deposit authorization form (my bank calls this an "automatic money transfer form"), instructing the bank to transfer the monthly total of your irregular expenses ($375 is the figure Sam and Samantha will use) from your regular account into your Freedom Account on a specific day of the month, preferably no more than five days after the date on which you will deposit your paycheck. Example: You are paid once a month on the fifteenth. You instruct the bank to automatically transfer $375 from your regular account into your Freedom Account on the twentieth of every month. The five-day "cushion" will cover the unusual months when your regular payday falls on a holiday or weekend. The selection of your transfer date is important, because once it's established, you can be sure the bank will never forget to make the transfer, nor will they be late.

STEP 4: *Get a loose-leaf notebook and label it "Freedom Account."* As far as the bank is concerned, you have a single account that you have designated your Freedom Account. (The bank doesn't care how you refer to it; banks recognize only account numbers.) But you are going to treat it as 6 subaccounts (or 3 or

8—whatever your particular case may be according to the number of irregular expenses you determined that you have; Sam and Samantha have 6). In your notebook (or on your computer, if you're one of those who prefers to automate your life), prepare one page per subaccount similar to Sam and Samantha's "Auto Maintenance/Repair" account (Figure 8.1). Keep it simple. Fill in the title, enter the amount to be deposited into that particular subaccount in the upper right-hand corner, and prepare five columns for each subaccount: "Date," "Description," "In," "Out," and "Balance."

STEP 5: *Get in the habit.* Each time you deposit your paycheck into your regular account, deduct the amount of your irregular expenses' monthly allocation ($375 for Sam and Samantha) on your regular account checkbook register. Don't even think about forgetting; the bank never will. It will feel weird in the beginning. You won't like making this debit entry because you'll think of so many things you could do with the money. But you are controlling your money instead of letting it control you.

Next, go to your Freedom Account notebook and enter the individual deposits. Here is how Sam and Samantha will make their first $375 automatic-transfer deposit into their Freedom Account: they will deposit:

$75 into Auto Maintenance/Repair

$60 into Auto Insurance

$40 into Life Insurance

$50 into Property Taxes

$100 into Vacation

$50 into Clothing

$ per mo. <u>$75</u>

AUTO MAINTENANCE/REPAIR
(ACCOUNT NAME)

Date	Description	In	Out	Balance
05/08/02	Opening deposit	$75		$75.00
06/08/02	Deposit	75		150.00
07/08/02	Deposit	75		225.00
08/07/02	Deposit	75		300.00
09/03/02	Check #101—Lube & Tune		29.95	270.05
09/08/02	Deposit	75		345.05
10/08/02	Deposit	75		420.05
10/15/02	Check #102—Zippee Tire Sales		156.72	263.33
10/16/02	Check #103—Auto Save—Battery		48.93	214.40
10/17/02	Check #104—Al's Big Tow		45.00	169.40
10/17/02	Check #105—Eddie's Electrical—Generator		143.20	26.20
11/08/02	Deposit	75		101.20
12/08/02	Deposit	75		176.20
01/08/03	Deposit	75		251.20
02/06/03	Check #106—Auto Save (20 qts. oil)		19.54	231.66
02/08/03	Deposit	75		306.66
03/08/03	Deposit	75		381.66

Figure 8.1

In the first few months of this new behavior, you must not give in to the temptation of making withdrawals from your Freedom Account for anything other than the purpose of the subaccounts. No borrowing. Don't dip into your "Life Insurance" subaccount to pay your monthly utility bill—even if you promise to pay it back. You may feel coerced, you'll be tempted, you'll be afraid you can't stop yourself, but don't.

At times you will also be tempted to think of this account as a savings account, and you may find yourself skipping your true savings or even hesitating to write appropriate payments out of the Freedom Account. This is not a savings account. This money has been committed already. The account will give new meaning to the phrase *ebb and flow*. It is strictly a financial-management tool.

Next month you will repeat this process. On the day you deposit your paycheck, you will go right to your regular account checkbook register and deduct the automatic transfer. You will then go to your Freedom Account, enter the individual deposits, and calculate the new balance for each of your subaccounts. The total of all your subaccounts in this second month should be two-twelfths of your annual irregular expenses. For Sam and Samantha, it is $750, or $375 times two.

Continue this procedure every month. In the third or fourth month, something wonderful will happen if you are diligent and don't give up: you will begin to experience a new level of comfort and tranquility. You will feel yourself starting to relax.

Here's what happened to Sam and Samantha Example shortly after they set up their Freedom Account. Sam had been trying to ignore a nagging guilt that he hadn't had the oil changed in the family car for far too long. They just didn't have the extra money, and it became something easy to ignore. Sometime during month 4 of their new Freedom Account, it clicked in Sam's brain: *Aha! "Auto Maintenance"!*

He ran to the Freedom Account notebook and found they had a balance of $300 in the "Auto Maintenance/Repair" subaccount (4 months × $75 = $300). He grabbed the Freedom Account notebook and drove to the Lube & Tune and asked for the $29.95 special. He entered $29.95 in the "Out" column of the "Auto Maintenance/Repair" subaccount page, wrote out check number 101, and calculated the new balance, $270.05. He couldn't believe how good it felt. The Freedom Account had just worked.

Upon leaving work late on October 14 (two months later), Samantha was greeted by a flat tire. Rats! Just what she needed. Payday was still two weeks away, and she knew the spare was not in good shape. All the way home she "sat light" because she was so nervous about riding on the spare. And she worried about how she and Sam were committed to incurring no new debt. But she obviously had an emergency. And then it hit her: *Aha! "Auto Maintenance"!* They'd become good managers of their money, and an emergency like this was exactly what they'd been preparing for! She arrived home with a smug grin on her face and scoured the newspaper to see what sales she could find on tires.

Early the following morning Sam headed for Zippee Tire Sales and purchased two new tires for $156.72. He wrote out check number 102 and calculated the new balance of $263.33. It actually felt good!

Sam bounded out to the car that evening feeling quite perky with those two new paid-for tires and all, got in, turned the key. Click, click, click . . . *nothing!* Dead battery. Oh, no! First the flat tire and now this! What else could possibly go wrong? But it didn't take long for the good news to sink in. *Yes! The "Auto Maintenance" fund!*

He walked a few blocks to Auto Save, where he found a good deal on a forty-eight-month battery—it was just $48.93. The Freedom Account could certainly handle the costs. He wrote check number 103 for a new battery. He entered the transaction in the Freedom Account notebook on the "Auto Maintenance/Repair" page, calculated the new balance to be $214.40, and proceeded home, slightly ticked off but nonetheless thankful for the Freedom Account.

The following day being Saturday, Sam and Samantha decided to load the family in the car and head for the zoo. Halfway there and for absolutely no good reason, everything died—again! What was going on? The Example family was miles from a service station, and nobody in the car had any mechanical ability.

However, they simultaneously exclaimed, "Aha!" and no one even came close to the panic stage. They had no choice but to call Al's Big Tow, which charged $45 to haul them to Eddie's Electrical Shop. The kids thought it was pretty cool. Sam handed Al check number 104 for $45 and figured the balance to be $169.40 just in time to meet Eddie, who quickly determined that the generator was shot and needed replacement. The bad news was the cost of $143.20. The good news was that they had plenty to cover the item. Samantha wrote Eddie check number 105 for $143.20 and calculated the new balance of $26.20, and they were on their way to the zoo.

Sam and Samantha faced four auto-repair situations within a three-day period. However, they were able to keep their cool, they paid in full for each item, and what would have normally been considered crises did not derail the Examples. They had actually prepared for those kinds of inevitable repairs. In the future, as they become more comfortable with their Freedom Account, they will be able to head off these repairs by practicing *preventive* maintenance. They will begin to assess tire wear, battery life, and generator performance before the parts are completely shot. By the way, looking at the Examples' Freedom Account, you will notice that Sam had a major awakening in February 2003. He figured that if he changed the oil himself, he could save money and afford to change it more often, which is probably the single most important auto-maintenance activity he could perform.

He took advantage of a great sale and purchased twenty quarts of oil (check number 106, for $19.54). He could no longer justify spending $29.95 to have it done when he could do it himself for less than $10 per change. In his pre–Freedom Account days, the small difference between having it done and doing it himself didn't seem to matter much. Things really have changed for the Examples.

How would Sam and Samantha have handled these situations a year ago, in their pre–Freedom Account days? First of all, they would have seen each incident as a major crisis, and the result would have been stress, bad moods, yelling, and fretting. They would have bemoaned their bad luck and blamed the stupid car for preventing them from getting ahead. Because they wouldn't have had any more money in their regular account than they do now, they would have felt forced to do one of the following: break out the plastic and hope they had enough available credit to cover the emergency; call Mom and Dad for another bail-us-out loan; write a hot check and hope the merchant didn't investigate it before they could get the heck out of there; or find some high-priced, underqualified auto-repair joint that would accept their department-store card. You laugh, but I think you're beginning to understand.

Other Things to Keep in Mind

A SLOW AND EASY START. I suggest that in the beginning you set up your Freedom Account to handle the minimum number of essential irregular expenses. If you are too aggressive at first, the system will require a large monthly transfer, and depending on your cash situation, you may be setting yourself up for failure. Start out simply and then gradually ease into expanding your Freedom Account.

OTHER IRREGULAR EXPENSES. Some items are not as predictable as auto maintenance/repair or property taxes and have a way of hitting us over the head when we can least afford them. For instance, an excellent way to keep insurance premiums low is to carry higher deductibles. But what happens if you are in an auto accident that requires you to fork over your $1,000 deductible? Ouch! That presents a huge problem for those who live paycheck to paycheck. I would advise adding a new subaccount to help with such potentially expensive emergencies.

INSURANCE DEDUCTIBLES. This Freedom Account subaccount should grow until its balance is equal to the annual deductible of your health, homeowner's, and auto deductibles. If you are nervous about raising your deductibles in the beginning, go ahead and start a subaccount, and when its balance reaches the amount equal to your current low deductibles, increase them so that you will pay lower premiums. Imagine the peace of mind you will have knowing that the deductibles are in place, ready to be used if necessary. If they are not necessary, the account is drawing interest. That is freedom. Once your subaccount reaches the amount you determine is adequate to cover your deductibles, you as the manager of the account are free to divert future deposits into some other subaccount.

CLOTHING ACCOUNT. You cannot imagine how many families do not list "clothing" when asked to outline their expenses. But they don't walk around naked or even wear tattered clothes. Just the opposite. I have noticed that those in the worst financial shape are often the best dressed. Where is that money supposed to come from? Many, of course, load huge clothing expenses on credit cards or write checks using funds that were supposed to pay for groceries or utilities. With a Freedom Account, clothing becomes a legitimate monthly expense. You may want to set up a general "Clothing Account" for the entire family, or three separate accounts: "His Clothes," "Her Clothes," "Kids' Clothes," or some combination thereof.

CHRISTMAS/HOLIDAY ACCOUNT. Probably nothing in the world throws more of us into a debting depression faster than approaching the month of December. Broke! And every January you say that next year you are going to save a little bit every month for Christmas. And do you? Well, lest I sound like a broken record, your Freedom Account is the perfect way to join your own Christmas Club.

DREAM ACCOUNTS. What is it that you hope to have enough money to do or be someday? Perhaps you'd like to take a class, redecorate the master bedroom, go on a special trip, start a stamp collection, or take up skiing. If you are like most of us, these desires remain dreams to be fulfilled "when we get some extra money," which is never. Well, not anymore!

The Freedom Account is how you will realize your dreams. Let your mind run wild. Insert new pages in your Freedom Account notebook and title them accordingly: "Redecorate Master Bedroom," "Room Addition," "John's Woodworking Tools," "Caribbean Cruise," "Sam's Dream Account," and "Samantha's Dream Account." Maybe you won't be able to start funding them right now, but little by little you will realize your dreams, thanks to your Freedom Account.

The Freedom Account is also a fabulous marriage-enhancing tool. By having individual accounts, both partners can manage some of their own money without feeling a need to sneak around or wallow in self-pity.

UNSCHEDULED INCOME. This is any money that comes into your life irregularly or unpredictably, such as rebate checks, tax refunds, freelance payments, gifts, and so on. You receive unexpected and unpredictable money all the time. It may be only $1 here or $10 there, but what happens to it? You put it in your pocket, and it is absorbed into your daily spending so fast that you hardly remember getting it. Larger amounts, such as tax refunds and consulting payments, usually go into the checking account with the intention that they will be used in some special way, but before you know it, the money is gone. And who knows where?

The Freedom Account is a wonderful solution to the problem of vanishing funds. Making a habit of depositing unscheduled income—big or small—into the Freedom Account and selecting the subaccount to which it will be credited suddenly give new meaning to surprise money. Let's say that you misjudged your federal tax withholding and end up with a refund of $1,000. If you put it into your regular account, it will disappear and eventually slip through your fingers via the ATM machine or some other phantom maneuver. But if you immediately put it into your Freedom Account, you will be able to decide which dream to nourish.

Common Questions about a Freedom Account

Q: Have you lost your mind? I don't have extra money every month to fund anything, let alone a Freedom Account.

A: Listen to yourself. You are acting as if maintaining your auto is optional or you can skip paying your insurance if you're a little short on cash. Do you really have a choice of whether or not to pay your property taxes or buy a few new work clothes? You are driving a car, your taxes were paid, and you dress fairly well. Exactly how did you do that? You came up with the money somehow, and you probably have a few credit-card payments that help you remember the trouble you went through to do it.

The Freedom Account is not a place to squirrel away extra money. It is a planning device to set aside money for expenses that will inevitably arise. You will pay for these expenses one way or another. This way, you don't constantly have to scramble and sweat to figure out how to meet the expenditures.

This step is too important to pass off as something you cannot afford. I suggest you start out with the bare minimum number of accounts, limiting them to your most essential irregular expenses. You may have to reduce your spending in other areas in order to get started with a Freedom Account, but whatever the sacrifice and no matter how painful it may be, this is one of the nicest things you will ever do for yourself.

Q: Won't setting up a Freedom Account bring me new, unnecessary expenses, such as fees for checks and service charges?
A: Yes. However, remember that as your total balance (the balance the bank sees is the total of all of your subaccounts) grows beyond the minimum amount required, all service fees will be waived. You will be writing very few checks from this account, so check costs will be minimal. I suggest that you choose your favorite subaccount (in my case, it would be "Decorating" or "Vacation") and designate it as the account from which you will deduct any "administrative" charges. However, this favorite account will also be credited with all of

the *interest* your Freedom Account earns. If you succeed in finding a bank that pays interest on checking accounts, you will make some good money that will be a great bonus for your favorite subaccount. Granted, the Freedom Account balance will fluctuate over the course of a year, but you are adding to it every month; this has a positive effect on your average daily balance. In time you will earn a nice sum of reportable interest, which should give your favorite account a boost and more than offset any costs incurred.

Q: How do I balance the Freedom Account each month?
A: Add up the current balances of the subaccounts. They should match the bank statement's closing balance once you have made allowances for checks that haven't cleared and deposits not yet posted. Balance it just as you would any other checking account. If you've never done this, step-by-step instructions can be found on the back of your monthly checking-account statement. Now, in the event you are at all like me and break out in a rash at the very thought of mathematical calculations, don't panic. A kind employee in the new accounts department of your bank will be more than happy to teach you this surprisingly simple process.

Q: Couldn't I create my own Freedom Account at home without opening up another checking account?
A: Sure. You could label a series of envelopes and put cash into each one every month. But the problems with this approach are obvious: This money is not designed to cover your monthly expenses. As the fund grows, you will be keeping larger and larger sums of cash—not smart from a security standpoint; you'd need a home safe or vault. Also, it would be too easy to engage in impulsive borrowing. If things got a little rocky, you might be tempted to skip a month or two. The Freedom Account should

be a serious business activity. To make it work, you have to be committed to it. If you're at all like me, you need the discipline and pressure of an automatic withdrawal. It puts everything on a much more businesslike, professional level. Besides, you probably won't pay yourself interest as the bank or credit union will. Record keeping is easier, too, because you will have canceled checks at tax time. (Some banks and credit unions no longer return canceled checks in monthly statements, which is another reason for duplicate checks.)

Q: What happens if my Freedom Account gets too large? Shouldn't I be investing the money?
A: Remember, this is not an investment vehicle; this is a money-management tool. Most of your subaccounts will be self-eliminating since you'll be drawing money out of them as you incur expenses. So you will never have continuously high balances. Subaccounts such as insurance deductibles or other items that may not be self-eliminating should have a cap. For instance, your insurance deductibles may total $1,000. Once you have reached the designated amount in your "Deductibles" subaccount, discontinue deposits until you must make a withdrawal. If you set up the Freedom Account properly, it is not going to present you with a problem of surpluses. Besides, I would hardly call that a problem. You will be amazed at how financially functional you'll become once you have the opportunity to manage your money.

Q: In the beginning, when the subaccounts have low balances, what will I do if I have an expense that is greater than the current balance in that subaccount?
A: Ideally you should find a way to open each subaccount with a larger initial deposit to cover this situation. Example: You open

your Freedom Account on October 1. Your semiannual property-tax bill is due on December 10. If your monthly property-tax deposit into the Freedom Account is $75, you will not have the $450 necessary to make the payment. You will have contributed only $225 total (3 × $75) to that particular subaccount. You should make an initial deposit into the subaccount to jump-start the process. By contributing an additional $225 to the account on October 1 to anticipate the shortfall, the problem would be solved. As you set up the Freedom Account, you might see where a few hours of overtime or a moonlighting position for a few weeks would raise the funds necessary to launch your Freedom Account in such a way that you'll be fully prepared for the first expense. However, even if you can't manage the additional funding in the first month, don't let this become an excuse not to get started.

Let's look at another scenario. Say you have a $75 balance in your "Auto Maintenance" subaccount and you incur a $150 repair item during the first month. What do you do? Write a check out of your Freedom Account for the $75, and supplement the balance from your regular account. Do not borrow from other Freedom subaccounts. While it pains me to suggest it, if you have absolutely no other way to come up with $75 (try hard—I mean *really* hard), I feel it would be better this one last time to put the balance on a credit card and then pay the credit-card payment from the "Auto Maintenance" subaccount. I recommend this only if the borrowed funds can be repaid within the following thirty days.

Example: Your "Auto Maintenance/Repair" subaccount has a balance of $75. Your repair bill is $150. You write a check for the $75 from the Freedom Account and pay for the balance with your credit card. By the time the bill comes, you will have made another $75 deposit into the "Auto Maintenance/Repair" subaccount, allowing you to write a check from the Freedom Account to pay off the credit card in full without incurring an interest charge. Going through the steps of depositing into the Freedom Account and writing a check to cover the $75 credit-card bill is necessary in order to keep everything straight and your subaccount page correct.

Accept the fact that it will take a little time to get the Freedom Account working smoothly. Don't let a little rough water in the beginning convince you to abandon such a wonderful, life-changing tool.

9

THE PRINCIPLE OF RESTRAINT

How to Live Within Your Means

It's time to start drawing your monthly financial blueprint. I prefer not to think of this as preparing a budget. Quite frankly, to me the word *budget* sounds confining and depriving (kind of like *strait-jacket* and *diet*). Instead, we're going to develop a *plan*.

Think about it: Great things are done with plans. Battles are won, houses are built, gold medals are won. So, rather than force you to wriggle into something that is about as well suited to you as another person's prescription eyeglasses, I'm going to help you custom-design your own Monthly Spending Plan.

Remember that in chapter 4 you started a new habit of keeping Daily and Weekly Spending Records? Now is the time to pull them out. You'll need them to create a Monthly Spending Record, which will lead into the ultimate Money Makeover tool—the Monthly Spending Plan.

So far we have determined that the key to balancing your finances is to start giving, start saving, stop the debt spiral by repaying debts quickly, and prepare for irregular expenses with a Freedom Account. Now you need to take control of the day-by-day spending that seems so out of whack.

You will need a few tools in order to get started: a pencil, pad of paper, and calculator. If you want to get really fancy, you can pick up a ledger or budget book at an office-supply store or dust off that financial software or spreadsheet program you bought for your personal computer. Any of these things will be of great assistance in drawing up this blueprint.

Step 1: Determine Your Average Monthly Income

Regardless of your payroll schedule or the frequency with which you receive other sources of income, you must come up with your average monthly income, the number that when multiplied by twelve equals your annual gross income. You will be working with gross—that is, before-tax—figures.

(Note: If you are self-employed as an entrepreneur or commissioned salesperson, don't think this chapter cannot apply to you. However, you may wish to jump ahead to chapter 10 to learn how to determine your average monthly income before going further in this chapter.)

When figuring out your average monthly income, include all sources of income, such as salary, wages, dividend and interest income, child-support payments, and alimony, using before-tax figures. If you get this money on a regular basis, can predict its arrival, and can spend it, then it's income.

Here's a quick formula for determining your average monthly income if you receive it other than once a month:

Weekly:	Multiply your weekly income by 4.333
Biweekly:	Multiply your biweekly income by 2.167
Semimonthly:	Multiply your semimonthly income by 2
Quarterly:	Divide your quarterly income by 3
Annually:	Divide your annual income by 12

Why should you use pretax income figures? Because everything withheld from your taxes represents "expenses" that you are obligated to pay, even though some of the deductions may well be for savings or retirement plans. These are expenses just like your rent and groceries, and it is important that you begin to recognize them as such. Your health-insurance premiums and all of the other amounts that keep showing up as deductions on your pay stub are expenses you pay. Some of the deductions may be optional, meaning you have the ability to eliminate or change them, but they're still expenses.

Let's go back to your income. Once you have come up with your accurate average monthly income figure, write down that number. We'll be using it later.

Step 2: Make a List of Your Expense Categories

You have fixed expenses (car payment, rent, mortgage payment, etc.) and flexible expenses (food, gasoline, telephone, utilities, etc.). Refer to the List of Possible Expenses Categories section on pages 107–110 to help you remember *every* way that you spend money. This is an exhaustive list of every type of expense I could think of, and it is divided into main categories and subcategories. Just pick out the ones that apply to you. You might want to use the main categories ("Housing," "Transportation," etc.), or you might want to go into more detail. You can combine categories or add new ones. The point is that your list of expense categories should be unique to you and your family. Do not repeat any of the categories that have already been listed in your "Freedom Account" notebook or Rapid Debt-Repayment Plan. Instead, list "Freedom Account" as one category and "Rapid Debt-Repayment Plan" as another. Be sure to include categories for savings and giving.

Try to be neither too detailed nor too general. Too many categories will be unmanageable; too few categories will give you only a vague idea of where you are. I recommend that the average family have ten to twenty categories on its Monthly Spending Plan, including the four mandatory categories of "Savings," "Giving," "Freedom Account," and "Rapid Debt-Repayment Plan." Don't forget to include categories for federal and state tax withholding, Social Security, and other payroll deductions. We often fail to take into consideration these major expenses when looking at our total financial picture. I suggest you have one category for taxes (state, federal, and Social Security, which is also referred to as FICA) and then another category, "Other Withholding," to handle everything else.

To make sure you haven't forgotten anything, take a look through your checkbook register, payroll stubs, and paid-bills folder to see how you spent your money in the last two or three months. Take note of your ATM withdrawals. (Do you have any idea where that money went?) This whole exercise should help you come up with an idea of your typical monthly expenses.

Step 3: Draft Your Monthly Spending Plan

Get a sheet of paper, or set up a computer spreadsheet, and make up a form using figure 9.1 (pages 104–105) as your guide. Transfer your expense categories to the Monthly Spending Plan form. Using the past as an indicator, fill in the "Plan" column across from each category with the dollar amount you plan to spend in each category during the next month. The "E/O" column is where you will honestly indicate whether this expense is essential or optional. Make sure that you do not combine any essential expenses with optional ones when you make up your category list. You may need to do some real soul-searching when you make this determination for each entry. For example, I know you probably prefer to think of cable TV and your cellular phone as essential expenses. Trust me, they aren't. Mark them "O."

When you have finished filling in an amount for each category, calculate and enter the total of your planned spending. Now fill in your average monthly income. Take a deep breath, go get a glass of water, and compare the two figures ("Plan" column total and "Average Monthly Income").

If your planned spending is more than your income, perhaps we have begun to uncover the root of your financial problems. If your "Plan" column came in less than your income, go on to the next step. If it is not less, now is the time to decide what you are going to do about this situation. You cannot go on spending more money than you have each month.

Since you have determined to stop relying on credit to cover your regular expenses, and since allowing your bills to become delinquent is no longer an option, you must find ways to reduce your regular monthly expenses.

Go back over each category, one by one. You may need to eliminate some of your optional entries for a while. Small sacrifices will reward you well in the future. You know you cannot mess with the Freedom Account (unless, of course, you have included sub-accounts that represent optional spending and could be eliminated for the time being) or your Rapid Debt-Repayment Plan. Your new commitment to these areas of planning ahead and paying off debt is absolutely essential to your Money Makeover. You will probably need to redraw this initial Monthly Spending Plan many times until you get it just right.

Sometime before the first day of the month for which you have designed this Monthly Spending Plan, you should have things organized. Let me assure you that your plan will be in a constant state of change, so don't feel defeated if you don't get it exactly right in the first few months.

Step 4: Activate Your Monthly Spending Plan

From now on, you will look at each month as having four weeks, regardless of what day of the week the first falls on or how many total days are in the month: days 1–7 will always be week 1; days 8–14 will be week 2; days 15–21 will be week 3; days 22 through the end of month will be week 4. It doesn't matter that the fourth week of every month will have anywhere from six to nine days.

Step 5: Count and Record Expenditures

As the month begins, it is necessary that you and anyone else who spends the family's income agree to keep a written notation of how the money is spent. This is not difficult, but it is extremely necessary. *Every expenditure*, no matter how small, must be accounted for and recorded from now on. Here's how you will do it: As you spend during the week, write down two things: "How much" and "What for." Every time you spend cash or write a check, you must record it. At the end of each week, tally up all expenditures for the week and record these totals by category in the appropriate "week" column on your Monthly Spending Plan. You may find yourself reworking your categories when, for example, you can't figure out in which category to record "Newspaper—35¢."

Step 6: Face the Month-End Truth

On the last day of the month (which will always be the last day of week 4), fill in the last column, "Wk. 4," with your expenses from week 4. Run individual category totals across and enter the amounts in the "Actual" column. Did you go over or under your "Plan" amount in each category? Enter the difference in the "+/−" column.

Now total the "Actual" column, adding up what you actually spent in all categories. How does this compare with your "Plan" column?

Let me predict what happened during the first month: (1) You had expenditures for which you had prepared no categories; and (2) you spent far more than you had planned and found yourself hopelessly broke and dying to write a bad check in week 4. Failure to acknowledge your true expenses is the reason you have lost control of your finances. You didn't mean to overspend—you were simply unaware of your true expenses! I hope you have a lot more insight now than you had a month ago.

Here's the beautiful thing about a Monthly Spending Plan: you are in charge! As a good manager, you need to start planning immediately for next month.

Step 7: Rethink Optionals

A logical place to cut expenses is in the area of nonessential items. Perhaps canceling cable TV or mowing the yard yourself might be in order for a while to reduce expenses. Maybe you've been indulging in luxuries that you really cannot afford at this time. (See chapter 11, "Cheap Shots," for many ideas for cutting expenses.)

Step 8: Prepare Next Month's Spending Plan

This is going to be easy because you have all the figures from last month. As you fill in the "Plan" column, use the data from last month's "Actual" column to give you a starting point. Look at your flexible categories, such as "Food" or "Utilities." How much could you reasonably reduce these items in the coming month? How much do you need to reduce spending in this area next month in order to come in under plan? Plug in a figure, and then do everything you can to reach the goal.

A Monthly Spending Plan is absolutely mandatory if you want to achieve financial independence. It doesn't take time; it saves time. It doesn't prevent you from having the desires of your heart; it takes you from dreams to reality.

Living with a Monthly Spending Plan

From now on, you will have two basic financial tools—your checkbook and your Monthly Spending Plan. This is where it gets a little tricky, but as long as you understand the function of each, you should not have a problem.

You must live according to your Monthly Spending Plan. For instance, perhaps you have designated $200 as your planned spending in the category "Groceries" for the month. You need to spend no more than $200, just as the plan states. However, your income may ebb and flow through the month, and if you have a current balance of $4.32 in your regular account, you'd best not run out and purchase $200 in groceries simply because that is the amount you have allotted on your Monthly Spending Plan!

You have based your Monthly Spending Plan on your *average monthly income*. Because your paycheck and other sources of income may not arrive on time, you may need to adjust and fine-tune the timing of your spending to accommodate your "cash flow." At times you will need to delay expenditures so that you do not move ahead of your deposits.

On the other hand, in some months your actual income may be significantly greater than your monthly planned spending. This is when you will need all of the discipline and restraint you can muster. Your common sense will tell you that the balance in the checkbook is not some newfound windfall. While I know that a balance of any significance in your regular checking account may not be something you're familiar with, get familiar with it. If you work your Money Makeover right, this will happen, so keep your hands off it! Your *average monthly income* has not changed; don't live as though it has.

You remember figuring "averages" in math class, don't you? You added up a list of numbers; some were small, others were large, but when you added them up and divided the sum by the total number of entries in your list, you ended up with the average.

The same principle is true of your income. Some months your actual income will be one of the smaller numbers in the list; other months it will be a larger one. But if you spend the excess or the amount over the average because you see a balance in the checking account, you are going to be in big trouble next month or the next. For example, let's suppose that you make $36,000 a year and that you're paid every other week. Your average monthly income is $3,000, but ten months a year you get two paychecks totaling $2,769.23, and two months a year you get three checks totaling $4,153.85.

Perhaps it's time to force a little financial maturity upon yourself. It's okay to have a balance in your checking account. It will not burn a hole there—just don't touch it. Allow your Money Makeover plan to work. Believe me, it will all come out right by the end of the year if you are patient, diligent, persistent, and disciplined.

I encourage you to take the simple Monthly Spending Plan and expand or enhance it so that your makeover becomes uniquely yours. I don't know what will work for you on a day-to-day basis. Perhaps you will want to use envelopes or coffee cans to keep your spending straight. I don't want to tell you how often to go to the grocery store. I do know what works for me, but it may not work for you. (We grocery-shop once a month, buy in bulk—and make it last. At times we've shopped for two months, which presents a whole new twist when living by a Monthly Spending Plan.)

Optimize your growth by consciously focusing on restraint. In the past, lack of restraint has caused you to make some foolish purchases, for which you may still be paying. Restraint is good, because it allows you to bring into action all of your intelligence and reason (which were ignored when you lived impulsively and made off-the-cuff financial decisions).

On the following pages, you will find a hypothetical Monthly Spending Plan for our friends Sam and Samantha Example. Remember, this is hypothetical and in no way suggests a perfect scenario. Use it as an example for creating your own plan.

You will notice that the Examples' savings and giving amount to about 5 percent of their gross income. While not optimum, this is a healthy start. Please keep in mind that the "Giving" category reflects only cash contributions and does not reflect nonmonetary gifts of time or talent.

You may be curious as to why the Examples have so few categories on their plan. This is the beautiful thing about having a Freedom Account and a Rapid Debt-Repayment Plan. None of the expenses covered in these two areas needs to be repeated. The simple entries "Freedom Account" and "Rapid Debt-Repayment Plan" take care of it. Clothing, entertainment, and medical/dental

MONTHLY SPENDING PLAN
MONTH OF AUGUST 2002

Category	Wk. 1	Wk. 2	Wk. 3	Wk. 4	Actual $ Spent in Mo.	Plan $ Spent in Mo.	Amount #+/−	E/O
Savings	100		100		200	200	—	E
Giving	100		100		200	200	—	E
Freedom Account	375				375	375	—	E
Rapid Debit-Repayment Plan	619				619	619	—	E
Mortgage Payment			850		850	850	—	E
Car Payment		172			172	172	—	E
Gasoline	18	21	16	15	70	80	−10	E
Groceries	70	72	78	65	285	300	−15	E
Food (Eating Out)	35	27	14	40	116	75	+41	O

Utilities			155		155	180	−25	E
Telephone				24	24	37	−13	E
Federal and State Taxes	816				816	816	—	E
Other Withholding	256				256	256	—	E
Baby-sitter	10			10	20	25	−5	O
Kids' Allowance		20			20	20	—	O
Newspaper/Magazines	3	5	6	2	16	20	−4	O
TOTALS	2402	317	1319	156	4194	4225	−31	

Average Monthly Income (see p. 95): $ 4,583.00

Total Actual $ Spent This Month: $−4,194.00

Underspent (or Overspent): $389.00 (underspent)

Figure 9.1

expenses will not have individual categories on the Monthly Spending Plan; instead, they will be handled in the Freedom Account.

Notice that the Examples underspent by $389 in August 2002. They are living beneath their means. I would recommend that they leave this balance in their regular account as a cushion. Eventually, if this excess continues on a regular basis, they should increase their savings allotment and devote the rest to their Rapid Debt-Repayment amount.

Two years from now, when they have completed their Rapid Debt-Repayment Plan, the Examples will immediately have $619 "extra" each month. What should they do? Their choices are many.

They could open a "New Car" subaccount in their Freedom Account and fund it to the tune of $619 each month; they could split that amount between several existing Freedom Account subaccounts; or they could start prepaying their mortgage by that amount each month. They could expect to pay off their home mortgage in record time with that kind of healthy prepayment of principal.

The wise management of our money gives us wonderful options, and that's what a Money Makeover is all about!

List of Possible Expenses Categories

The following list includes all possible living expenses I could think of. Some of these are not monthly expenses and so would need to be included in your Freedom Account. Others are either regular monthly expenses or categories in which you have frequent but not necessarily regular expenses. Remember, this list is only a guide. You must set up your categories in the way that best fits your situation.

GIVING

Church/synagogue   Charities

FREEDOM ACCOUNT

RAPID DEBT-REPAYMENT PLAN

HOUSING

Mortgage payment   Rent

TRANSPORTATION

Licensing/registration   Inspection
Gasoline   Parking
Oil/antifreeze   Public transportation
Tires   Other
Repairs

GIFTS

Birthdays   Wedding/baby
Anniversaries   Christmas/holiday
Business-related   Other

UTILITIES

Electricity   Heating oil
Water   Telephone
Gas   Wireless phone

Online service

Cable TV

Trash pickup

CLOTHING

Adult

Children

Laundry

Dry cleaning

Other

RECREATION/ENTERTAINMENT

Vacations

Shows/movies

Sporting events

Dining clubs/parties

Hobbies

Other

PERSONAL/HOUSEHOLD

Furniture

Kitchen appliances

Utility appliances

Electronic appliances

Linens

Utensils

Computer and printer
supplies/maintenance

Tools

Beauty shop and sup-
plies

Barbershop and sup-
plies

Fitness center

Toiletries

Reading material

Pets and supplies

Veterinarian

SAVINGS

Contingency fund

Investment

College

Retirement

Other

HOME MAINTENANCE

Maintenance

Grounds care

Other

MISCELLANEOUS

Tuition

School supplies

School room and board

Athletic fees

Union dues

Professional fees

Licenses

Lessons

Other

FOOD

Groceries

Business lunches

Fast food

Restaurants

School lunches

Other

MEDICAL

Medicine/drugs

Dental

Eyeglasses

Doctor and dentist visits

Medical insurance

Dental insurance

Hospital costs

Other

INSURANCE

Auto

Life

Property-casualty

Renter

Other

SUPPORT/CHILD CARE

Alimony

Child support

Day care

Baby-sitting

Support of parents

Children's allowances

Other

TAXES (WITHHELD)

Income (federal)

Income (state)

Social Security (FICA)

Other

OTHER PAYROLL WITHHOLDING

Supplemental health
    insurance

Disability

Unemployment
    insurance

How to Live Within Your Means

If your efforts to design a Monthly Spending Plan that fits within your income have left you with a three-alarm headache and a feeling of defeat, take heart. You are not alone, and there are remedies. If you are determined, nothing can stop you. But there are no instant solutions. This process takes time. You must never give up. Eventually you will be able to look back and see in amazement that step by step you were able to completely change the direction of your life.

There are only three ways you can change the numbers on your Monthly Spending Plan:

1. Increase your income.
2. Sell your assets.
3. Decrease your expenses.

1. INCREASING INCOME. This is probably the first thing most of us consider when facing financial hardship because it appears to be the quickest and most painless solution. However, of the three remedies listed above, I believe this is the least desirable. Increasing income does nothing to address the root problem of habitual overspending and poor money management. More money just provides more opportunity and greater ability to overspend, and allows the debt-prone individual to qualify for more debt. Increasing income invariably increases expenses in the form of taxes, child care, transportation, clothing, and meals out. It takes a great deal of additional income to realize a substantial net effect after all the tax collectors have taken their share.

Consider the effect that increasing your income has had in the past. Think back five years. You have increased your income since then, so why wasn't that the solution?

2. SELLING ASSETS. This is an excellent way to make a onetime or occasional adjustment in your Monthly Spending Plan, provided you have assets with resale value. The best way to find out if you do is to make a list of everything you own. Take each item and assign it a market value, the amount you could reasonably sell it for within the next ninety days. (This is not a bad exercise to go through once a year, even if you have no intention of selling anything.)

Next, go through your list and rate each item according to these criteria:

- Things I don't want to keep
- Things I could live without
- Things I can't live without

You might be amazed at the total market value of all the stuff cluttering up your home and your life that you could easily live without. Every day people just like you are getting extra cash by selling things they no longer use or need. I suggest you cautiously decide what you have that you can actually live without. Don't make hasty decisions, or you may live to regret selling something you still need.

Holding a garage sale is an excellent way to liquidate low-priced goods. For more valuable things, consult with an antique dealer or consignment-store owner. Perhaps your area has an auction that accepts the kinds of items you wish to sell. Look through your local classified ads to see what price others are asking for similar goods. Study the ads to see which ones are the most appealing. Let your friends and neighbors know of anything you have for sale. Your best customer might be right under your nose.

Money realized from selling assets can be used in several ways: to speed up the Rapid Debt-Repayment Plan, or to deposit the funds in one or more subaccounts of your Freedom Account, thereby reducing the monthly withdrawal from your regular account. Selling assets is a good way to raise your income, but not many of us can count on hosting a successful garage sale more than once a year or so. However, using the proceeds to pay down debt will have a permanent net effect on your bottom line. If you apply the proceeds to meet your regular monthly expenses, the result will have an effect only in that month.

3. DECREASING EXPENSES. Cutting expenses is by far the most desirable way to live within your means. Example: If you

work overtime in order to earn an additional $100, you will be lucky to see $50 that you can apply to your Monthly Spending Plan. However, if you cut $100 from your monthly food bill, you will instantly see a $100 net effect on your Monthly Spending Plan's bottom line month after month.

Decreasing expenses has many other benefits that make this by far the quickest and best way to get your income and your expenses in line. By forcing yourself to pay attention to what you are spending and to find ways to spend less, you'll increase your consciousness about spending, you'll become a better steward of what you have, and you'll be better able to see which things in life really matter. You'll become more appreciative by waiting until you can purchase something with cash. You'll find yourself more flexible, and you'll travel through life with a spring in your step rather than a pain in your neck!

The idea of reducing your living expenses to 80 percent of your income might seem impossible right now, but it's not. We humans are amazing creatures. How few our true needs, how vast our wants! The trick to achieving this reducing act is in assessing your present situation, deciding what percentage of reduction must take place, and then proceeding to work on every area accordingly. It can be done. You have a new mission in life: save money any way you can!

There are literally thousands of ways to cut your expenses. However, until you have a plan and a way to measure the effect of cutting expenses, it seems meaningless to save $1 here when you are in a major financial crunch. To be honest, it seems as frustrating as trying to drain the ocean cup by cup. This kind of frustration may prevent you from making any change in your spending habits. But when you have a clear-cut Monthly Spending Plan, these savings multiplied over and over will make the unbelievable possible.

Four Tricks of the Trade

1. Ask yourself tough questions. Because you are going to become increasingly conscious of every penny you spend (you will be writing it down), you can train yourself to approach spending in a new way. From now on, before you make a significant purchase (you decide what "significant" is—perhaps anything over $20), stop and ask yourself these questions:

Do I really need this? If the answer is yes, go on. If the answer is no, bravo! You just saved yourself from a stupid purchase.

Do I already have something that would do just as well? If the answer is yes, you've just saved yourself money. If the answer is no, go on.

Could I find a cheaper substitute? If the answer is yes, don't buy now. If the answer is no, go on.

If after applying this little test, you find that you still need the item, that you don't have anything else that would do just as well, and that you need all the quality you can afford, go ahead and make your selection. And then? *Wait* for a full twenty-four hours—a full week is far more desirable—until you actually make the purchase. End result? If you go through with the transaction (and you won't believe how many times you'll change your mind during the mandatory waiting period), you will never wonder if it was the right thing to do.

2. As much as possible, live with cash. When I refer to *cash*, I mean full payment up front—no credit cards, no bad checks, no games, no manipulation.

For a long time, the only way I could guarantee that kind of honest transaction was to pay for everything with actual dollars. I was too crazy with a checkbook, and credit cards were out of the question. I have, however, become quite responsible with a business checking account over the past few years and can even be trusted with our personal checkbook. I haven't bounced a check in nearly fourteen years! In some ways, I have become obsessive about balancing the checkbook on a daily basis. It works for me, so that's what I do. But for day-to-day, nonbusiness purchases, I use cash. I haven't been mugged and don't even worry about it because I carry so little cash at any one time.

I recommend that anyone with an overspending problem chuck the checkbook and credit cards and depend on cash and/or money orders. This will put the brakes on the insanity of spending money you don't have. And my experience is that if you force yourself to live with cash, you will spend less because it forces you to be a much more careful consumer. Try it the next time you go to the grocery store. Leave the checkbook at home and take just the amount of money you have allotted for groceries.

3. *Never buy better quality than you need.* For example, if you need something for a single use, you might be wise to buy the cheapest thing you can find or to rent it. But when it comes to something like a mattress, which you want to last for many years and consistently give you a great night's rest, you would be well advised to buy the highest quality you can possibly afford . . . with cash.

4. *Never buy new until you have considered used.* The secondary market in this country for everything from auto-

mobiles to zithers is absolutely astounding. I'm not saying you should never buy anything new; just consider buying used before possibly paying five to ten times as much for new. You're going to love what that kind of transaction does for your Monthly Spending Plan.

The wonderful thing about living within your means is that as you practice saving and giving, as you assess your true needs and put your wants and desires into proper perspective, and as you plan for the future, your anxiety level diminishes and abundance begins to flow—abundance in the form of contentment and joy as well as money and material things. The balance is rewarded. I can't explain it. I just accept it.

As Your Means Change

Now is the time to determine how you will handle increases or decreases in future income. In the past you failed to plan for such occurrences. As your income increased, you hardly noticed it because of all the overspending you were doing. When it decreased, the bottom fell out of your world.

Using Sam and Samantha as an example, let's say that Sam receives a 10 percent salary increase on January 1. If they have not planned ahead for such an occurrence, it is likely the Examples will head into the new year with a false sense of having $5,000 extra to *spend*. And what about the new income Samantha will be generating from her home-based desktop publishing business? Without the security of knowing exactly how to handle these increases in their income, they could easily be deceived into believing they can go out and buy all kinds of neat stuff. On the other hand, what if Sam gets laid off and has a ninety-day period of unemployment?

I know this is going to sound like an old broken record, but you must start with step 1 and go right on through. And step 1 was? Determine your average monthly income. So back to the planning board you go, adjusting figures so that you come up with your new average monthly income.

Next, you must go to your Monthly Spending Plan and start adjusting. Savings need to be increased or decreased to reflect the new income base. The figures for "Giving," "Taxes," and "Other Withholding" must be adjusted to account for the increased income or lack thereof.

Once these adjustments are made, leave your spending plan alone for the time being if the adjustments were caused by an increase in income. Give your new situation three or four months to settle in. If you see that you are consistently spending well under your income, readjust.

Perhaps now would be the time to increase your entertainment allotment, increase your deposits, add new subaccounts to the Freedom Account, or boost your Rapid Debt-Repayment monthly allotment. The key is that as your income increases, you respond cautiously and slowly. Don't blow it by jumping into outrageous new debt.

Eventually, as an experienced financial manager, you will know when you're ready to take on a larger mortgage or higher rent. You'll know when it's the right time to buy another car (with cash) or take the cruise you've been dreaming about.

And if the adjustment is due to a *decrease* in income? Then you need to go right down the list and adjust the figures according to the percentage drop in income. It could be a bleak picture, or if you have been diligent in paying off debt, you might be pleasantly surprised at how flexible you have become.

The key is finding balance and planning ahead. Determine beforehand exactly how and what you will adjust if and when your income changes. It may well go up, and then, on the other hand, it could go down. The steps in adjusting your Monthly Spending Plan will remain the same.

10

DIFFICULT SITUATIONS

What to Do with
Less-than-Tidy Circumstances

Even if you follow the Money Makeover plan that I've outlined, you still might encounter problems and situations that trip you up. Let's take a look at some of the difficult situations you might find yourself in.

No-Fault Financial Problems

Not everyone's financial situation is a result of poor money management. Perhaps your troubles stem from huge medical bills not covered by insurance. Maybe you are a single parent trying to survive on a below-poverty-level income. My recommendation is that you follow the principles of the Money Makeover as much as possible, and then not be ashamed to seek assistance from outside sources. In this country, charitable organizations and governmental agencies might be able to help you. Of course, your best tactic is still to find new ways to cut expenses.

Self-Employment

If you look to commission sales or other forms of self-employment as your sole source of income, the words *roller coaster* probably bring more to mind than a large steel edifice at Six Flags Over Somewhere. And I would not be surprised if because of your status, you have dismissed most of what you have read thus far as inapplicable to your situation. Having been self-employed most of my working years, I know exactly the justifications for being unable to plan ahead or stick with a plan.

The majority of those who fall into the irregular-income category live in constant uncertainty. Some months can produce absolutely no income. Then a deal closes or a big account comes through, resulting in a good-sized check, which usually is applied in its entirety to catching up. During those particularly wonderful months, the entitlement mentality kicks in, demanding that something extravagant be purchased. Somehow when the big deal closes, we forget about the lean months and the fact that there may be many more ahead.

The phrase *Feast or famine* sums it up. For many, at least in the beginning, self-employment means survival on a daily basis. "Self-employeds" usually conclude it is impossible to come up with any kind of reasonable spending plan or to live within one's means when the means are so unpredictable. But this is wrong!

Commissioned salespersons, freelancers, and small-business owners make a huge mistake when they fail to become their own strict and unbending employer. Those of us in this position must wear two different hats—that of employer and that of employee.

As the employee, you need to determine honestly what is the lowest reasonable amount you can accept from yourself, the employer, as monthly compensation. Now that's a new twist. Usually, self-employed people ask, "What is the largest amount I can possibly pull out of this business every month?" Let's say, for example, that your rock-bottom, absolutely minimum figure is $3,000 a month, based upon your Monthly Spending Plan. You may intend to bring $10 million into the business this year, but determining your reasonable monthly requirements has nothing to do with that. As your employer, you must determine if the "business" (this applies to commissioned salespeople, too, who should see themselves as self-employed) is able to commit to this $3,000 monthly salary for its favorite "employee." Let's assume that it can.

Next, you must open another checking account. If you are a typical small-business owner, you take varying sums of money (depending upon current need or availability) directly from the business account and deposit them into your personal checking account. The amount probably fluctuates greatly from month to month. As a freelance artist or commissioned salesperson, you have been used to depositing your commission checks or payments directly into your personal account. This is a problem!

By opening another checking account, you will be able to take control. Example: You receive a $10,000 commission check in January, nothing in February, and nothing in March; in April you receive four checks for $550, $1,200, $3,000, and $850, which is not so bad. That's $15,600 for four months, which should more than cover your expenses of $3,000 a month. The problem is, in January you might have had to play catch-up on all of the holiday bills that you couldn't pay because December was a "dry" month. And then there were all of those great after-Christmas sales, and you felt as if you had extra money so you splurged a bit here and there. Along come February and March and no income. The personal checking account is depleted, the credit cards are called into action, and it's desperation time until April. The $5,600 received in April barely gets you caught up, and so goes the ride on the roller coaster.

With the new checking account method, here is what would happen: the January $10,000 check would not be deposited into the regular checking account. Instead, it would go into the holding account (or whatever you want to call it). You would become a strict and stern employer and guard this account as any good employer or business owner would. On "payday"—that is, a predetermined day on which you pay yourself each month—you write yourself, the employee, a paycheck for $3,000, regardless of the balance in that account. After all, as your own employee you can't expect a raise every month. It's $3,000 (or whatever the amount you have previously negotiated with yourself) on payday, and that's it. On February 1, you write yourself a $3,000 paycheck. On March 1, you write yourself a $3,000 paycheck. On April 1, you deposit the $5,600 and write yourself a $3,000 paycheck, and so on each month.

If your self-employment work is sufficient to support you and your family, you should not have to worry. The income flowing into the holding account should exceed the paychecks. As the holding account becomes healthy, additional funds will be available to carry you through lean times. When things are going well and you have sufficient reserves, you might even consider sitting down with yourself to negotiate a raise, but don't be too hasty. Weigh the pros and cons. Consider the position of the prudent employer and the needy employee.

The self-employed person's major problem is the temptation to live it up when a big check comes in. After all, surely a bigger and better deal is just around the corner, and the extra income will take care of the future. You seem to be living within your means, but don't be deceived. Your success as a self-employed person lies in your ability to discipline yourself and be a fair, but strict, employer and at the same time a grateful, restrained employee.

Negotiating with Creditors

What happens when one's financial situation becomes so dire that even after doing everything we've discussed (keeping impeccable spending records, setting up a Freedom Account, cutting expenses to the bare minimum, and incurring no new debt), ends still don't meet? What happens when there's nothing left to cut, no hope of increasing income, and no more assets to liquidate?

The following suggestions are for only the most desperate situations. Unless you have honestly tried every tactic to bring your spending in line with your income and kept impeccable spending records for at least four months, you probably shouldn't even be reading this.

This advice is for those critical situations in which declaring bankruptcy seems to be the best alternative, but you are willing to try one last possibility.

Look at your list of debts. No doubt they are killing you. Minimum monthly payments may exceed your total income. By now these creditors are sick of hearing your stories and promises, and you're just as sick of hearing their threats. Perhaps you've been avoiding their calls, allowing their collection tactics to ruin your day and throw you into depression.

Look back at your Monthly Spending Plan. Aside from your Freedom Account and Rapid Debt-Repayment Plan, what is the total of your *essential* monthly expenses? (I assume that you have cut this to the bare bone, and that this number represents only your basic needs.) When you deduct these expenses from your average monthly income, how much is left? Maybe you don't have enough left to commit to even the minimum monthly payments to your creditors listed on your Rapid Debt-Repayment Plan. If it isn't enough to pay these minimum monthly payments, how close is it? To find out, divide the amount of money left over after paying for essential monthly expenses by the total of your minimum monthly debt payments. That will give you a percentage. Let's say for illustration purposes it is 60 percent. You can't pay 100 percent of your monthly payments on your debts, but you can pay 60 percent.

I am not about to propose that any of your creditors waive payments. I'm suggesting that given the right set of circumstances, your creditors might be willing to work with you to renegotiate the terms of your payback. But you must approach them in a mature, sincere, and responsible manner, and you may have to ask forgiveness for your own past behavior.

First, you need to look deeply into your heart. Are you willing to keep whatever promise you make to your creditors? If you cannot embrace integrity as part of your new makeover, you will not succeed.

None of this is going to be easy. I hate confrontations, and you probably do, too. My knees get weak and my voice trembles when I have to make difficult phone calls. I find writing letters to be easier, but not always as effective.

Look at your Rapid Debt-Repayment Plan. First, take each of your minimum monthly debt payments and multiply by the percentage you can pay. Next, contact each of your creditors and tell them, "I have a real financial problem. I don't want to declare bankruptcy. I've entered into a financial-recovery program. I have come up with a plan that I am dedicated to working with and a repayment plan to which I am committed. I do not want you to suffer, and I am determined to pay back every single cent I owe you. I intend to pay you 60 percent [or the percentage you have determined] of my current monthly payment. I promise to pay you the same amount every month even if my required minimum payment drops. I need your help."

I have provided a sample letter (below) that would be appropriate to send to each of your creditors. Feel free to use it verbatim on one condition: you must be willing to carry through and make every promised payment. This is a serious letter, and you should not use it without a great deal of thought.

The letter ends with an "assumptive close." You are asking for a favor and acting as if it has been granted. You must enclose a check or money order to demonstrate your good faith and commitment.

Creditor Name
Creditor Address
Date

RE: Account
Dear Sirs,
I [or we, as appropriate] am writing to you about my account as referenced above. I deeply regret that I have fallen behind and have failed to abide by the terms of our agreement. I want you to know that I am committed to full repayment in the amount of $_____ .

I have recently undertaken a financial-recovery program and have assessed my financial situation, and as a result, I have created a full repayment plan. I am doing everything I possibly can to avoid filing for bankruptcy.

Your account, unfortunately, is only one of the many that I owe; my total debt is $_____ , with monthly payments totaling $_____ . You can understand that my present net *monthly income of $_____ , less drastically reduced living expenses of rent, food, utilities, etc., does not leave funds sufficient to pay even the minimum monthly payments to which I agreed.*

Enclosed please find my check in the amount of $_____, which represents the amount I will be able to pay each month on my account for the next six months. At that time my situation will be reviewed. I hope the payments will be increased regularly to allow for total repayment at the earliest possible date.

I respectfully request that the interest rate you are charging be reduced so that a greater portion of my payment will go toward principal reduction. Further, I request that during this recovery period, when you are accepting these lower payments, you do not report this account as late to the credit bureaus as long as I make these new payments on time.

My financial-recovery program projects that I will be completely debt-free within _____ years.

I look forward to learning that you have processed this payment in acceptance of my request. If, however, you are unwilling to work with me as outlined above, kindly return the enclosed payment so that I can send an additional payment to another of my creditors who has agreed to the plan.

Thank you in advance for your cooperation.

Sincerely,

I hope that each check or money order enclosed with these letters to your creditors will be cashed. In my opinion, the fact that the payment was accepted indicates the creditor has agreed to your offer. You may continue to get phone calls, however, so receive them courteously.

Keep your recovery program and your commitment to full repayment uppermost in your mind. Whatever you do, don't miss a single payment and don't be late. After six months, contact your creditors again. Let them know how the plan is going, and tell them if you will be able to increase the payment.

Some people have had great success with this approach, while others have encountered creditors who don't want anything to do with renegotiating. But don't let one negative response defeat you. Send that creditor another letter in a week or two. Change the words, but don't change the message. Send it to the supervisor or the president of the company with an explanation that although your offer has been turned down, you are sure management will rethink this response. Be courteous but persistent, persistent, persistent.

Bankruptcy

Some financial situations are beyond repair. In these situations, few choices exist besides filing for bankruptcy. While bankruptcy can offer a fresh start for some, it can also turn out to be a ten-year mistake if filed in haste or without sufficient cause.

Do not think about filing for bankruptcy until you have considered and exhausted all other options. Once you have filed, it will be nearly impossible to get credit or rent a home or apartment. Many who have taken such a drastic step describe themselves as "financial lepers." Don't believe anyone who tries to convince you this step will be easy or a joyful way to start over.

Before filing for bankruptcy, it is always advisable to contact Consumer Credit Counseling Services (800-388-2227) to find the office closest to your home and get a second opinion. You may find you have a viable alternative through CCCS or some other qualified debt-management organization.

If you decide to file, shop for a reasonably priced bankruptcy lawyer who will explain the pros and cons. I would be suspicious of anyone who tried to convince me it was all good and easy.

There are two forms of personal bankruptcy: the wage-earner plan and straight bankruptcy. Under the wage-earner plan, called Chapter 13, a court trustee supervises the full or partial repayment of your debts, usually over three to five years. Under a straight bankruptcy, or Chapter 7, the court apportions most of your assets among creditors. Federal law, unless overruled by stricter state limits, lets you keep up to a certain limit of home equity, household goods, auto equity, and other limited assets.

Many people who go through bankruptcy find a sense of relief, but the inevitable emotional toll should not be underrated. Bankruptcy will be on your record for life. Accept that. Even though it may drop off your credit report in ten years, you will still have to answer truthfully whenever you purchase real estate or engage in other major transactions and are asked, "Have you ever filed for bankruptcy protection?"

If you must choose to declare bankruptcy, remember that nothing prevents you in the future from repaying the creditors you have harmed. If God chooses to grant you the means in the future, I believe it would bring great honor to His name for you to go back and repay your debts.

No matter which way you choose to go, I hope that you will learn from your past experience and not go back to living beyond your means. Believe it or not, after filing for bankruptcy, you will become what some creditors consider a good risk. They will try to load you up with new debt because they know you can't file again for bankruptcy for a number of years.

Your fresh start should include living by the principles of this Money Makeover. They will help you to get started on the right course and to stay out of trouble.

During these difficult times, take care of your relationships. Don't underestimate the impact of bankruptcy on your spouse and children, both as part of the family and as individuals. You will all more than likely need to go through the stages of anger, guilt, and grief. In some ways, it will be like facing a death.

But don't lose hope. There is a new tomorrow, so pick yourself up, dust yourself off, and start all over again. Take courage from this letter-writer, who obviously stumbled badly but managed to regain her footing—and learn valuable lessons along the way.

There I was, a young single mother lacking direction, without child support, and battling depression. I took my daughter and moved to another city, hoping to escape an abusive ex-husband.

I lived on credit as long as I could and ran up such a mess I figured my only solution was to file for bankruptcy. I saw this as a way to wipe the slate clean and treated the whole mess as part of the past. I figured I was entitled to a fresh start.

I found a way to get a whole new identity and a new set of credit cards, and did I ever use them! I thrived on the instant gratification they offered. Eventually, I started my own business, which really sped up my debt-making abilities. I worshiped money and just couldn't get enough of it. It was my anesthetic of choice and deadened all the pain I was facing in my personal life. At one point I had ten separate checking accounts.

I began buying real estate. At last I had found my niche, and no one was more surprised than I at my newfound business success. I learned to use every leveraging tactic known to the business world to mortgage myself into oblivion. I became a magician at juggling accounts, payments, and refinancing.

During the height of my career as a real-estate tycoon, I married a wonderful man. He married an image, and believe me, I had created some image! Within a short period of time after we were married, I could no longer keep up the juggling act, and my house of cards crashed. My new husband got to meet the real me.

We had no choice but to file for bankruptcy. I cannot describe the humiliation, the pain, the shame, and the disgrace of going through bankruptcy again—and this time dragging my new husband along with me. I hurt him, I hurt many other people, and I destroyed valued friendships.

The difference this time, however, is that we did not attempt to fix things by ourselves. I've taken full responsibility for what I've done, and I'm willing to learn from past mistakes. We no longer live to keep up an image. By turning our lives over to the control of God and applying sound financial principles to our lives, we have been able to pick up the broken pieces and put things back together. We have begun a formal savings plan, we pay our bills on time, and we've been able to buy a home. My priorities have completely changed as I am learning to discern what is important and what is not.

Filing for bankruptcy twice is something that I am ashamed of. However, in some odd way I am learning to be thankful for that, too, because as a result I am finally learning how to be financially responsible and content.

—Hydee

11

CHEAP SHOTS

Hundreds of Ways to Cut Expenses

In your lifetime, you and your family will probably purchase an entire fleet of cars, thousands of items of clothing, tons of groceries, and numerous insurance policies. You will drive millions of miles, repair and replace many major appliances, eat thousands of restaurant meals, and help keep several utility companies in business. With a little planning and a lot of determination, there is no reason you should pay full price for any of these goods and services.

Now that you are committed to living well on 80 percent of your income, it is critical that you s-t-r-e-t-c-h every dollar to its absolute maximum, and there's no better time than right now to get started. Besides, when you learn to scrimp in unimportant areas of your life, you can splurge where it counts. You can't begin too soon to reduce your expenses and improve your life.

Food

Never shop when hungry. Your hunger will override your good intentions every time! Stick to a list prepared ahead of time. A little discipline never hurt anyone.

Learn to cook and bake from scratch. Get out your cookbooks and be brave. You'll save a lot of money, you'll eat more nutritiously, and you just might enjoy it. Come on—if I can do it, anyone can!

Shop with cash. You will be a much more careful shopper knowing that if you go over your limit without a checkbook or credit card to fall back on, you will be embarrassed at the checkout counter.

Use coupons carefully. Very carefully! Some slick marketing program is hoping against hope that you will clip and cash in. Use coupons only for items you would normally buy even if you didn't have the coupon and only if it is truly a savings. Check other brands that might be on sale or are already cheaper. Manufacturers often offer coupons as incentives to buy new products or luxury treats. But you're not saving anything if you're suckered into it.

If you do have a qualified coupon, buy the smallest size allowable. You'll usually save a higher percentage of the purchase price by buying the smallest size.

Find a market that will double the coupon's value. This practice varies throughout the country, but if you do have good coupons, make sure you find a way to double them. Some stores even triple them on certain days.

Shop less frequently. You will be forced to make the food last longer, and you will become more creative. Start by doubling the time between trips. If you go to the market every day, stretch it to every other day. Once a week? Shop for two weeks next time. You'll waste less, use less, and spend proportionately less.

Don't shop at convenience or specialty stores. You won't find any bargains there. Specialty items are expensive, and you can find quality substitutes at your regular or discount supermarket.

Stretch fruit juice. Mix fifty-fifty with generic-brand club soda or seltzer.

Drink water. Your doctor will love you and so will your food bill. Keep a pitcher of chilled water in the fridge. Rave about its wonderful qualities to your young children. They'll think it's a treat if you are convincing enough.

Find a thrift bakery outlet. These stores generally have fresh products (not necessarily day-old) at cut-rate prices. Shop on special 10-percent-off days. Load up the freezer.

Make your own substitutes. Instead of buying mixes and ready-to-go cooking products—for muffins and cakes, biscuits and rolls, hot chocolate, and so on—watch for recipes and make your own.

Eliminate choices at meals. Stick to your plan and let your family know that from now on there will be only two choices: take it or leave it.

Leave the kids home when you shop. You will stick to your shopping list with much less frustration and stress if you fly solo.

Stick to the perimeter of your supermarket. That is where you will typically find the produce, meat, and dairy products. The center aisles are the prepackaged and preprocessed high-priced items, also known as the danger zone. Refuse to tread where you don't have to.

Buy the largest quantity rather than individual portions. Take soda pop, for instance. Cans usually cost more than bottles for some reason (unless you are using a coupon, in which case you have already learned to buy the smallest size allowable).

If your market charges for grocery bags, bring your own. Recycling is a pretty good habit to develop.

Change eating habits. Learn about the nutrition benefits of beans and rice instead of meat. Sneak in vegetarian meals. Experiment with legumes and grains—they are much cheaper and quite good.

Come up with creative menu titles for what otherwise might be considered plain and boring. Add your ideas to these suggestions: Baked Potato Bar; Chef Salad Night; Bits and Pieces (my kids' favorite meal when they were little, this is any combination of things in the fridge cut up to bite-size and cleverly arranged on a plate); Smorgasbord Night (a glorious array of this and that— leftovers that you couldn't even think of throwing away); Hors d'Oeuvres and Mocktails.

Shop at a discount warehouse store. You'll give up the glitzy ambience, but you'll save big! (Caution: Some have annual membership fees, so weigh the benefits.)

Learn to s-t-r-e-t-c-h. Oatmeal or bread crumbs stretch a pound of ground beef into a pound and a half or more; nonfat dry milk stretches a gallon of milk into two; borax and baking soda stretch automatic dishwashing detergent. The possibilities are endless.

Create cheap gourmet coffee. Break up a cinnamon stick into dry coffee grounds or add a few drops of vanilla extract to brewed coffee.

Buy in bulk. This will cut down your trips to the grocery store and will often save 50 percent of the unit cost. Reorganize your kitchen and pantry. Find places outside the kitchen to store dry and canned goods. Repackage large amounts into small units.

Become a shelf-life expert. Buying in bulk will do you no good if you end up throwing most of it away due to spoilage. Some things last indefinitely, while others spoil, even if frozen, after a certain period of time.

Use cloth napkins. Fine restaurants do. Make your own from sheets or other soft fabric. Just think of all the disposable products you could do without (paper plates, paper napkins, Styrofoam cups, plastic cutlery, paper towels).

Consider generic and store brands. Some generic items are awful, and others are exactly the same product as the name-brand alternative. Do some experimenting, especially if your store offers "satisfaction guaranteed." If you don't like it, the store may let you exchange it.

Make eating at home fun. Rearrange your eating area. Make a new tablecloth. Use place mats. Play background music. Light some candles. Have a picnic in the family room.

Plant a garden. You don't need major acreage to grow tomatoes, herbs, and an occasional row of lettuce. Consider the square-foot method or container gardening (go to your library for a how-to book).

Keep a price book. Start keeping a notebook that lists the prices of regularly purchased items at various stores. Refer to it when you see specials or ads to determine whether you're really getting a bargain.

Check the reduced and day-old sections of the store. But be sure to check the expiration dates. No buy is a good buy if you have to throw the item out.

Avoid shopping on the first of the month. Some stores have been known to raise their prices during the time welfare and Social Security checks come out.

Shop during mark-down time. Ask the butcher or produce person when he or she marks down items. You'll be surprised how helpful this can be, and you'll get the best of the sale items.

Don't shop when you are exhausted. You will not be as disciplined or effective.

Watch for refunds and rebates. Be careful. Your time is precious, but if you can fit it in, there's money to be made.

Make your own pizza stone. This is the key to professional-quality pizza. Instead of paying $30 for a commercial pizza stone, pick up an unglazed terra-cotta tile at your local hardware store for about a buck. Place it on the lowest rack in the oven, heat up the oven to four hundred degrees, and bake the pizza directly on the tile.

Always use powdered dry milk for baking. If a recipe calls for cream or condensed milk, use only half the usual amount of water you would use with the dry milk.

Use paper coffee filters several times. Just carefully rinse them off between uses.

Make your own salad dressings and croutons. You will save at least 50 percent.

Reserve eating out for special occasions. Restaurant and fast food will cost you at least double. Consider eating out as an occasional treat.

Weigh all produce, even if it is priced per item. You won't believe the difference in weight of the prebagged carrots, for instance! Even with a weight printed on the bag, the real weight may be quite different. Heads of lettuce priced individually can differ in weight by as much as half a pound! Get the most for your money.

Go to a farmers' market. You can buy fresh fruit and vegetables at great prices. Some cities hold these markets only in the warm months; in other areas, they're held year-round.

Buy produce in a bag for the best value. Watch out: often the bruised and spoiled fruit will find its way into the bottom of a bag. So pick out the best bag.

Load up on loss leaders. These are the advertised sale items that the store uses as bait to get you in the door. Buy all that you can reasonably use and that will still fit into your spending plan.

Store cartons of cottage cheese and sour cream upside down in the fridge. They will keep twice as long.

Cook in cast-iron pots. Doing this boosts the iron content of food. Soup simmered for a few hours in an iron pot has almost thirty times more iron than soup cooked in another pan. Health is important in keeping down medical expenses.

Keep fish fresh and odorless. Here's how: Rinse it with fresh lemon juice and water, dry it thoroughly, then wrap and refrigerate it.

Make your own baby food. Check your library or bookstore for a how-to book. Freeze the food in ice-cube trays to make convenient individual servings, then store them in sealable bags. (Exceptions to making your own are formula for newborns and rice cereal.)

Clean out and rearrange your pantry often. You won't believe the stuff you'll find hiding in the back. (Check the expiration dates.)

Use frozen orange juice concentrate instead of ready-to-drink. It's cheaper, and it lasts longer.

Consider a vacuum-sealing machine. It makes buying in bulk much more sensible. But don't buy one unless you're sure you'll use it.

Get a freezer. Too expensive? Consider sharing space with a neighbor or friend.

Keep your freezer full. A full freezer is an efficient freezer. If you don't have enough food to keep it jam-packed, fill plastic jugs with water (leave room for expansion) and freeze them. You'll have fresh water in case of a power failure, and the frozen jugs will keep the freezer contents cold much longer.

Don't wash berries. They will freeze better if they aren't washed first. Any other washed fruit must be thoroughly dried before freezing.

Freeze strawberries whole. Remove leaves, but leave stems.

Use zip-type plastic bags for freezer containers. Squeeze out as much air as possible before zipping the bags closed.

Keep a written index of freezer contents. Hang the index in a handy location. This way you can spend as much time as you need looking through inventory to make a decision without having the door open and letting in hot air.

Freeze items quickly. When putting things in the freezer, spread them out so all sides are in contact with the cold. When they are frozen, move them together compactly.

Blanche vegetables before freezing. They contain enzymes that, if their action is not stopped, will cause the product to become coarse and flavorless. Enzymes defy freezing but cannot withstand heat. Before freezing, drop fresh vegetables into boiling water and transfer immediately into ice water. Work with small batches.

Properly wrap foods. Materials must be waterproof and moisture- and vapor-resistant to prevent food from drying out. Wrap very tightly, removing as much air as possible. Seal with tape.

Freeze these items:

ONIONS. Chop them, then spread them out in one layer on a cookie sheet. Place them quickly in the coldest place in the freezer. When they are frozen, transfer them to a bag or container.

MUSHROOMS. Do not wash mushrooms. Clean them with a bristle brush. Chop and freeze them in the same manner as onions.

BROWN AND POWDERED SUGARS. Freezing them prevents lumps.

COFFEE. Freezing coffee beans and ground coffee maintains their freshness.

NUTS. Freezing nuts retards spoilage. Nuts left in the pantry will become rancid.

POPCORN KERNELS. Freezing them keeps them fresh much longer and will encourage every kernel to pop.

MARSHMALLOWS, POTATO CHIPS, PRETZELS, AND CRACKERS. For the best results, freeze them in the original unopened containers.

Clothing

Don't pay full price. With so many manufacturer outlets, discount mail-order catalogs, and fantastic sales, you should never pay the full retail price.

Buy fewer, but buy classic. Rethink your wardrobe to include fewer pieces. Make the few pieces classic items that look great year in and year out. Stay away from trends or fads.

Coordinate. Stick to a basic color scheme so you can mix and match clothes to create more outfits with what you have.

Accessorize. Well-chosen accessories can turn the same basic dress or suit into four or five different looks.

Find a good tailor. Someone skilled at alterations can take in, let out, take up, let down, and redesign a classic and well-made garment.

Avoid "dry clean only." This kind of expensive maintenance will double or even triple the cost of a garment over the years.

Find a good, reasonable dry cleaner. Some cleaners charge a flat rate per item. Shop carefully. Use home dry-cleaning kits to extend the time between professional pressings and cleanings.

Repair, resole, and reheel shoes. You can easily double or triple the life of a good pair of shoes with simple repairs. Do the same with luggage, handbags, and belts.

Recycle. Instead of having your children wear their siblings' hand-me-downs, trade with neighbors or friends who have children of the same sizes. The kids get a new look, and the price is right.

Leave your good business shoes at the office. Change into an older pair when leaving to tromp up and down steps and out to the parking lot.

Shop at consignment stores. High-quality, previously owned clothes are sold at often 70 to 85 percent below the new price. Shop well, and you will find unbelievable bargains.

Check out thrift shops. Never buy just because it's a good bargain. But if you have the time, you might be able to save a lot of money there.

Wash with cold water. Unless you are dealing with unusual stains, cold water and good detergent will clean just as well as warm or hot water. You'll save on hot water, the fabrics will last longer, and colors will stay bright much longer.

Change your clothes. As soon as you get home from work, change out of your expensive business suit and into casual clothing to minimize the chance of stains and snags.

Rent, don't buy, formal wear. Evening gowns, bridal dresses, and other formal wear are usually high-priced—and worn once. So rent or, better yet, borrow. For men, tuxedo rental prices vary tremendously, so check around.

Stock up in the off-season. Seasonal items (swimwear, coats, boots, etc.) are often cleared out at phenomenal prices, so if you can handle the thought of buying snow wear in the spring, go for it!

Borrow maternity clothes. Start a co-op with your friends. Typically, maternity clothes don't get that much wear and are easy to maintain.

Become a stain-removal expert. Eliminating ugly stains may allow another year of wear. Use shampoo on collar and cuff rings. Shampoo is meant to clean body oil, which causes rings around collars and cuffs. Baby shampoo is an excellent substitute for expensive cold-water soap.

Sew buttons on once and for all. Use dental floss for thread.

Avoid shopping at the last minute. Start planning ahead for your clothing needs. Last-minute stress is costly.

Ladies, buy men's white T-shirts to wear under jackets. They're cheap, easy to dye or trim, and machine-washable.

Think twice about leather, suede, and silk. They are lovely but expensive to maintain.

Hand-wash delicates. Take them into the shower with you, and use your shampoo on them.

Household

De-junk your home. If you are like most people, you have about twice as much stuff as you really like, use, or need. Have nothing in your home that you do not know to be useful or believe to be beautiful.

Learn to make repairs. Few household repairs are dangerous. Read manuals, take classes, be brave, and tackle the things that are not going to endanger your well-being.

Measure detergent for both the washing machine and the dishwasher. If you just dump it in, you are probably using way too much.

Recycle. Find new uses for things that are about to exceed their normal life span. For instance, worn-out bath towels make terrific car-washing rags. Worn-out socks and diapers make good dusters.

Use shaving cream as an upholstery cleaner. It's effective and cheap. Use it to spot-clean small areas.

Buy queen-size top sheets for king-size beds. King-size top sheets are usually way too big and require a lot of tucking in.

Queen-size flats work great on most king-size beds and are a lot cheaper.

Buy sheets instead of yardage. Buying sheets on sale gives you extra-wide yardage at a fraction of the cost of yard goods. They're perfect for making curtains, tablecloths, napkins, pillows, night-clothes, and crafts.

Instead of buying finished area rugs, buy a remnant from a carpet store and have it bound. It's usually much cheaper.

Arrange for regular monthly bills to be paid directly out of your account by your bank. You'll save the costs of postage, late fees, checks, and envelopes.

Save receipts, warranties, and owner's manuals. Often these are all you will need to have an appliance repaired at no charge. Find a nifty binder that will keep everything neat and orderly.

Fire the maid. Get all the occupants of the house involved in cleaning. Learn speed-cleaning techniques.

Buy unfinished furniture. A little practice will go a long way, and usually the store will give you a quick lesson. Buy the finishing products from a discount hardware store.

Beware of home shopping by television. The products are highly overpriced and overrated and are pitched to the compulsive shopper.

Learn to shop without buying. A little attitude change will allow you to thoroughly enjoy lovely things but leave them in the stores. Let someone else dust, polish, and care for them. You can visit "your" stuff whenever you like and change your mind without consequence!

Get friendly with salespeople. They usually know when things are going to go on sale. Ask and then be willing to wait.

Rent carpet-cleaning equipment. Save big-time by doing this chore yourself. You can usually rent better equipment than you could afford to own.

Clean the garage or basement. Hold a sale and get rid of what you don't use so you can organize what you do use.

Read magazines and books to learn cheap home-decorating tricks. Picture framing, using sheets to make curtains and pillows, stenciling, and wallpapering are easy and fun. Check out the library for how-to books and publications.

Make your own cleaning products. Avoid the high-priced commercial products. Your library probably has several books that will tell you how to make environmentally safe and child-safe products.

Make dust cloths. Dip cheesecloth into a mixture of two cups of water and one-quarter cup of lemon oil. Let it dry.

Clean silk flowers. Pop them into a paper bag with a small handful of uncooked rice. Shake the bag to remove the dust. Throw out the rice (who knows what was hiding in those flowers?).

Don't clean paint-roller covers and brushes until your job is completely finished. Just wrap them tightly in plastic wrap overnight (or a couple of days) and keep them in the freezer. They'll stay soft and usable until you're ready to finish the job.

Store partially full cans of paint upside down. The paint will form an airtight seal, extending its useful life.

To remove ugly oil stains on your driveway, sprinkle it with kitty litter and scrub it with a brick. Repeat this process for stubborn stains.

Make your own household deodorizer. Put a cinnamon stick or a few whole cloves in the vacuum-cleaner bag to make your house smell clean and fresh. (This doesn't work unless you actually run the vacuum!)

Remove ink marks from plastic. Spray it with hair spray and wipe it clean.

Sharpen scissors. Cut through a piece of 220-grit sandpaper.

Utilities

Buy energy-efficient. When selecting a new appliance, look for the yellow tag with the "EER" on it. The higher the number, the less wasteful of energy and more efficient the appliance is.

Preheat the oven only if the recipe tells you to. Casseroles and roasts don't suffer from starting out cold.

Let your fingers do the walking, even if it requires a toll call. It's cheaper than driving your car.

Check to see if you have deposits on account. Usually if you have been a good customer (gas, water, electricity, phone) for at least a year, you can arrange to have your deposits refunded or credited toward your account. You may be able to get interest, too, if you ask.

If someone in your family has a vision impairment, try to get free directory assistance.

Take short showers instead of water-guzzling baths.

Install a flow-controlling showerhead. Your kids will never notice, but your water bill will.

If your phone service is interrupted for more than twenty-four hours, ask for a credit. You'll probably get it, especially if you nicely point out that you pay dearly for the privilege of having a telephone link to the outside world.

Always check for a toll-free number before dialing long distance. It's free to call 800 Directory Assistance (1-800-555-1212).

Close off seldom-used rooms. This way you don't have to heat them in cold weather or cool them during the hot months.

Conserve electricity by using a carpet sweeper (one of those push-type gizmos with brush rollers) instead of vacuuming every day. Vacuuming once a week will probably be more than sufficient for deep cleaning.

Substitute a fluffy comforter for your electricity-sucking electric blanket.

Put an egg timer by the phone. The timer will remind you to hang up before you talk yourself into debt oblivion.

Call corporate collect. Try it. Most large companies will accept your collect call as a matter of course. Just identify yourself as a good customer or potential client. If denied, just call back direct. Hey, it's worth a try, and it usually works.

Always ask for credit immediately upon dialing a wrong number. Don't be embarrassed. It's routine.

Have a phone checkup annually. Request an equipment inventory report. The phone company will send you a form listing the services for which you are charged. If you find you've been overpaying, demand a retroactive refund.

Consider having the telephone company block 900 numbers. They are never free and can cost as much as $20 a minute.

Turn off the oven or stove right before an item is completely finished. Whatever heat is left is usually enough to finish the job.

Use glass or ceramic for baking. If you use these kinds of dishes in the oven, you can lower heat by up to 25 degrees from what's called for by recipes.

Check that the stove burner equals the pan size. The pan should completely cover the burner to avoid energy waste.

Use three-way bulbs. They are more efficient provided you use the lower wattage whenever possible. Dimmer switches are good energy conservers as well.

Don't open the fridge or freezer until you are sure what you are going after.

Replace a cracked or loose gasket around the refrigerator door.

Run only a full dishwasher. Otherwise you're wasting precious hot water and electricity.

Don't leave the coffeepot warming for hours on end. Instead, transfer finished coffee to a thermos and turn that energy-sucker off.

Keep the water heater at about 120 degrees (midrange). The water will wash just as efficiently and will be less apt to scald.

Run the dishwasher in the evening and turn it off before the dry cycle. Open the door and allow the dishes to air-dry overnight.

Wrap blanket-type insulation around the water heater. The savings over the first year will probably more than pay for the blanket.

Draw drapes or close awnings to cut down on heating and air-conditioning. Drapes act as great insulators.

Put up storm windows and check the weather stripping around doors and windows. Anything you can do to make your home air-tight will reduce your heating and cooling bills.

Insulate your basement to prevent loss of heat and coolness. The cost should be recouped within three years.

Get a utility checkup. Many utility companies will send representatives to your home and give you free advice on how you can conserve energy better.

Use fabric wall hangings. A quilt or decorative rug will insulate interior walls and keep your room cozier with the thermostat turned down.

If you leave a room for more than fifteen minutes, turn off the lights.

Cook topside whenever possible. The stove or range top uses less energy than your oven.

Choose smaller appliances. Electric skillets or woks, slow cookers, and pressure cookers use less energy than a range or oven.

Set the refrigerator thermostat at 38 to 40 degrees Fahrenheit. This is probably about 10 degrees higher than recommended by the manufacturer but can cut running costs by almost 25 percent.

To get similar savings from the freezer, set it between 0 and 5 degrees Fahrenheit.

Vacuum the coils at the bottom or back of your refrigerator frequently to prevent dust from building up around them. Dust makes the refrigerator run more often and so does keeping it too close to the wall. The refrigerator and freezer need room to breathe or else they get too hot and run too much.

Turn off the curling iron, clothes iron, coffeepot, etc., when they are not in use.

When baking, keep track of the cooking time with a timer. Don't keep peeking into the oven. Each peek can cost as much as 25 degrees Fahrenheit; it can also affect browning and baking.

Install timers and/or motion detectors rather than leaving lights on all night. This will ensure you're using lights only when necessary.

Fill a small plastic bottle with water. Place it in your toilet tank away from the flushing mechanism. The tank will require less water, and your toilet will still flush just fine.

Buy your own phone. Renting from the phone company is very expensive.

Consider energy-efficient lightbulbs. They cost more up front, but you will save a lot over the long term.

Make sure your lightbulbs are the correct wattage for the appliance. Putting a 150-watt bulb in a 75-watt socket wastes energy, and it could cause a fire.

Reacquaint yourself with a clothesline. Hanging out a few loads of laundry each week instead of using a gas or electric clothes dryer can save hundreds of dollars each year.

Turn the water heater way down when you are away on vacation.

Install water-saving toilets when you need to replace your old ones. Check with your utility company. Many offer rebates in excess of the cost of a new commode just for your trouble.

Check for leaks. Drop a little food coloring into the toilet tank. If any color shows up in the bowl, you have a leak. Fix it.

Water your lawn at night. Sunshine encourages evaporation. If you water the lawn at night, more water will stay on the lawn and penetrate into the roots, allowing your watering time to be shorter than during daylight hours.

Close the fireplace damper unless you have a fire going.

Check out your phone bill. Phone companies are not perfect, and chances are you've been paying for someone else's phone calls.

Call during the cheapest hours. Usually nights and weekends.

Avoid directory assistance. It's amazing that phone companies actually charge for that, but they do. Get a phone book and use it.

Use postcards to communicate on nonurgent matters. They're much cheaper than a long-distance phone call.

Put your phone service on "vacation" while you are out of town. The savings are modest, but every little bit helps. It is less than cancelling service altogether but puts considerable restrictions on service while not requiring reconnection. It restricts outgoing calls. Check to see if your provider offers a "vacation" option.

Reconsider all the phone add-ons. Maybe you aren't even using some of the features you're paying for (call-waiting, call-forwarding, speed dialing, etc.).

Buy heating oil off-season. Start checking prices in the spring. Typically, you should be able to take advantage of lowest prices from July to September. The same applies to firewood.

Freeze before you freeze. This works only if you live in a cold climate. Putting room-temperature items in your refrigerator or freezer actually heats up the environment in there for a while.

During the winter months, put these items outdoors to cool before resorting to the fridge or the freezer.

Insurance

Take higher deductibles. In essence, you partially self-insure by being willing to take the chance that you won't get sick, you won't crash the car, and you won't be burglarized. The higher the deductible, the lower the premium. The insurance company actually compensates the customer who is willing to share a greater portion of the risk.

Commute by car pool. Most insurance companies offer discounts to low-mileage drivers.

Stay out of the death lane. The far left lane is where speeders hang out and most accidents occur.

Drive for five drivers: yourself and the drivers in front, at both sides, and behind you. Be prepared for them to do the unexpected.

Have adequate protection. With the higher deductibles, you can afford to get better coverage, which is a wise move.

Find a company that gives discounts for having all of your types of insurance with the same company. Insurance companies can offer volume discounts.

Call your agent every year. Make sure your agent has all of the correct information—including your teenage son's good driving record and three years' experience. All of these things might matter.

Install a timer on a radio or TV as well as on outdoor and indoor lights. Timers are cheap protection. Burglars tend to avoid a home if they think there's a chance someone's around.

Don't be predictable. A car that's always parked in the same place for the same amount of time each day or night lets thieves know where to look for it and how much time they'd need to make off with it.

Ask about discounts for security systems, smoke alarms, good driving records, etc. Always ask! The agent or company may not volunteer the information.

Add a replacement-cost rider to renter or home-owner insurance. Doing so may cost a little more, but in case of a claim, you will be glad you did. Without it, the company will depreciate the value of every item, and you will be a big loser.

Consider umbrella liability. It is very cheap and could be a lifesaver, especially if you have kids and your exposure is great. Check with your agent.

Don't make small claims. Too many can lead to policy cancellations or premium hikes. Insurance companies think that a frequent filer is heading for a serious accident.

File for diminution of value against the other guy's insurance company if the damage to your car was the other guy's fault. Even though it is repaired adequately, the car has a diminished resale value, for which you should be compensated. On average, you can file for 10 percent of the total repair cost. Be persistent.

Don't buy travel insurance. It's one of the biggest rip-offs.

If possible, pay premiums annually. Avoid the added costs for monthly or quarterly billing.

Don't put insurance policies in a safe deposit vault. These boxes are often sealed by court order when the box holder dies. That could cause a substantial delay.

If you're single, buy life insurance only if someone is financially dependent on you.

Scrutinize your deck sheet with every renewal. This is the coverage sheet that shows your limits. Don't overinsure. Computers have a way of sneaking stuff in.

Make sure you are with a highly rated company. These days the smaller, lower-rated companies are dropping out regularly. Better safe than sorry.

Buy term life insurance. Experts whom I trust advise that whole life and universal life are not wise investments. Check with your own professional—but do check.

Don't buy life insurance for kids. It makes absolutely no sense. Insure only wage earners (and stay-at-home moms!) whose death would create financial hardship.

Don't buy too much life insurance. Make sure it is adequate to maintain current lifestyles and needs. Don't let your agent decide how much you need. He wants to make a big sale! You decide. Insurance companies will say that a family needs at least enough life insurance to cover four or five times its yearly income.

Cut back on life insurance as your dependents become independent. Providing for a spouse alone costs less than a spouse and eight kids!

Never buy insurance from television or direct-mail ads. This is a sleazy marketing ploy. The premiums are at least 400 percent too high for the coverage, and the exclusions are mammoth.

Drop your comprehensive and collision insurance when the value of your car drops below $2,500. Save the difference in premiums to buy another car.

Videotape your home inside and out for insurance records. In case of a fire, you need to have evidence of the expensive wall coverings and decorator window coverings. While you are taping, narrate the scenes aloud and describe them in detail. Keep the tape in a safe-deposit box. Make sure the video date is well documented. Revideo the house every few years or when considerable changes are made. Tapes don't last forever either.

If you rent, buy a tenant's policy. This is a must. Landlords are not responsible for your belongings in case of disaster.

Never buy credit disability insurance, automobile service contracts, extended warranties on appliances and electronics, or Chargegard (for credit cards).

Never buy mortgage life insurance. This is the kind of policy tied to your mortgage or other credit purchases that will pay off the balance in case of your death. If you think you need the additional insurance, arrange it yourself, and leave your heirs the choice of paying off the mortgage or not.

Transportation

Think long and hard before buying a new car. Since financing charges are so great, paying cash is the method of choice, and new cars are expensive.

Research. Check *Consumer Reports* and other publications to learn all you can before making a decision.

Buy at a slow sales time. February is the best month to buy because consumers are worn out and dealers try to get their attention with sales. The second-best time is two weeks before Christmas. Terrible weather provides a good time to make a deal.

Choose a car not coveted by criminals. A phone call to your local police department will reveal which are the most-often-stolen cars in your area.

Don't carry more than you need. A light load gets much better gas mileage. Clean out heavy items from the trunk, and leave only the spare tire and safety equipment. Don't make your car a mobile warehouse for stuff you can leave in the garage.

Avoid roof and trunk racks. These things ruin aerodynamics and cut gas mileage.

Never drive when angry or upset. Angry drivers waste fuel, are dangerous to themselves and others on the road, and are hard on the engine.

Listen to traffic reports to avoid tie-ups and congestion. You may be able to change routes and avoid costly congestion.

Reduce warm-up time. A thirty-second warm-up is sufficient for modern cars. Any longer and you are just wasting precious fuel.

Be gentle and keep it steady. A light foot on the accelerator will certainly save fuel. Slow down. Not only will you get optimum performance, but you may avoid a costly ticket and unfortunate insurance increases.

Be diligent about regularly scheduled maintenance. It pays off every day. It makes parts last longer, prevents most emergency breakdowns, and promotes good gas mileage.

Be observant. Look, listen, and sniff occasionally for anything unusual about your car. You know your car best, and early diagnosis will pay off later. Take note of odd noises, hard starting, or significant loss of power.

Have your brakes replaced before the rotors have to be turned. You'll save hundreds of dollars. Your mechanic should check for free and tell you how much of the pad is remaining. Don't push it past 5 percent.

Check your own fluid levels. Just a little time and patience will go a long way to keep engine, brakes, and transmission in tip-top shape. Make sure you have a reliable teacher.

Learn how to do some of your regular maintenance. Books, videotapes, colleges, and adult schools all can teach you about routine maintenance. It's not so hard to fix a car—the hard part is figuring out what's wrong!

Find a professional you can trust to handle the major stuff. Don't be afraid to get a second opinion.

Check battery terminals. Corroded battery terminals can leave you stranded. Quick fix: pour a cola drink or other carbonated beverage over the terminals. It will eat through the corrosion. This is a temporary measure to get you where you need to go without a tow.

Keep tires inflated properly. Underinflated tires drag down gas mileage; overinflated ones cause premature wear. Don't forget to check the spare, too.

Buy the smallest car you can live with. Weight is the biggest enemy of fuel economy.

Keep your cars longer. Proper maintenance will allow you to keep a car for ten years or longer. My professional insists that if maintained right, a car should serve faithfully for more than 300,000 miles.

Use public transportation whenever possible. It's still cheaper than driving your own, especially if you are alone.

Rent. If you live in a big city with good public transportation, sell your car and rent one on the rare occasions when you really need one. You'll save on insurance, wear and tear, and parking.

Sell an extra car. Do you really need two, three, or four cars?

Pay cash for used. It makes much better sense than financing a new auto. Auto loans carry huge interest rates.

Skip the vanity license plates. Find a cheaper way to promote yourself and your causes.

Check on insurance rates before you make a decision. Call your agent with a couple of choices and get quotes.

Avoid fancy options. They just mean that there are many more expensive things to go wrong.

Try to get yellow rear-turn signals. Research suggests that cars with yellow turn signals are less likely to be hit from behind while turning than cars with red signals.

Never agree to buy a dealer's options. Extended warranties, fancy paint-job protectors, racing stripes, sun roofs—these are huge profit items for the dealer.

Don't lease. Leasing only encourages trading in more often. Even the best lease is going to cost you more in the long run.

Don't trade in your old car. Sell it yourself. The dealer will probably never give you what you can get for it from an individual buyer.

Drive with the windows closed. Open windows mess up aerodynamics and cost you more in gas mileage than running the air conditioner.

Pump your own gas. Full service is outrageously more expensive. Keep a box of disposable plastic gloves handy so you don't smell like a service-station attendant all day. Inspect your fan belts. Carry a spare or two in your trunk.

Wash and wax your car yourself or teach your kids how. Professional car washes are very expensive.

Buy oil and other fluids in bulk at the discount store. Buying oil a quart at a time at the service station is not smart.

Pay registration renewals on time. Most states hand out heavy penalties if you are even one day late.

If you rent a car, reject offers of additional optional coverage. Be prepared for some heavy-handed tactics to get you to accept it. Salespersons get hefty bonuses if you can be persuaded.

Don't throw away empty tissue boxes. They make wonderful caddies for the car. They are the perfect size to hold sunglasses, lotion, spare change, and cassette tapes, and they can be used as trash receptacles in the car. They are also good storage boxes for crayons, doll clothes, and puzzle pieces.

Home Owners and Renters

If you have an extra room, consider taking in a boarder to help defray your costs. Post a notice (for free) at a local community college or corporation. Check with personnel offices at larger corporations in your area. Often they assist employees in locating affordable housing.

Get more than one bid for major repairs or improvements.

Don't fall for scams. They usually come in the form of door-to-door salespersons.

Don't overbuild for your neighborhood. Usually, the most expensive house in the neighborhood appreciates the least.

Carefully choose location. Location is the most important criterion in selecting a home.

Drive a hard bargain when you purchase a home. Get help from friends or relatives, who will be less emotionally involved than you are.

Negotiate the closing costs. Always ask for more than you are willing to accept.

Make sure you earn interest on your deposit during the escrow period.

Never allow the seller to select inspectors. You want an impartial assessment of possible termite damage, roof condition, plumbing and electrical situations, and structural soundness.

Make sure the escrow holder is truly impartial. Often the seller's broker will steer the escrow to a company in which he or she has some financial interest. It is better to have an escrow with no ties.

Have your head examined before you attempt to build your own home. Unless you are a developer or professional contractor, you are in for a big surprise, not the least of which is that it could cost twice what you estimate.

Change smoke detector batteries on your birthday. Also, vacuum the detector to get dust and dirt out of the sensors. Smoke detectors don't last forever, so make sure you test yours often and replace it readily.

Move into a smaller house. The lower costs could drastically improve your financial situation.

Use students and other nonprofessionals for moving furniture, gardening, painting, carpentry, and any other odd jobs that you cannot do. Call your local college or university and ask for the job-placement office.

Sell by owner. Prepare for lots of aggravation and allow time to research and learn how. You can save a significant amount of money.

Shop your mortgage. Programs vary a great deal. Get many opinions.

Refinance your existing mortgage. If you plan to stay in the house for the next two to three years and you can beat your present interest rate by 1.5 percent, it may be a good idea. Consider the points on the new loan. Try to negotiate the closing costs and points if possible.

Pay more than the monthly payment. This is probably one of the best things you can do with extra cash. You will pay down the principal more quickly, which will result in a tremendous saving of interest.

Instead of paying your mortgage monthly, pay half of your mortgage payment every two weeks. You will end up making twenty-six half-payments, which equal thirteen monthly payments. Your spending plan will absorb this additional payment with little, if any, pain, and your principal will love you.

Do your own painting and decorating. Check out home-improvement centers to learn the latest techniques.

If you are going to sell your home at a loss, try and hold off a while and rent it out so that you can take advantage of the tax loss when you eventually sell. Check with your accountant. If you can show it as an investment rather than as a personal residence, you might be able to recoup some of the loss.

Challenge your property-tax bill. If your value has declined, you might be entitled to a reassessment of your taxes.

Clean out gutters. Be careful. It's a little tricky, especially with a two-story home. You may, though, prevent some drainage problems in the future.

Remember your onetime $125,000 exclusion on capital gains if you are fifty-five or older.

Check with your city. Sometimes low-interest or grant money is available for modernizing or fixing up the outside. Be the first in line.

If you have a home business, a portion of your mortgage and related expenses may be taken as a tax deduction. It's tricky, so get professional advice.

Install automatic timers on your sprinkler systems. Water less often for a longer period of time to allow deep penetration.

If you rent, find an area with rent control. If the law is in place, you might as well take advantage of it.

Get a roommate so you can afford a nicer, bigger place. Make sure to put in writing the details of your agreement about who pays for what.

Negotiate the rent. In a market where many vacancies exist, the tenant is king.

Be clear about your rental agreement before you sign anything. Deposits should be clearly spelled out. Ask for interest to be paid on the deposits.

Before you vacate, take extra pains to clean. No one wants a hassle over return of deposits. The landlord will give you a good recommendation in the future, and that is valuable.

Health and Personal Care

Get your hair cut, colored, or curled at a beauty school. Students are usually carefully supervised, conscientious, and anxious to please. Be nice, but firm, about your expectations and desires. Prices are unbelievably low.

Take advantage of store testers and free samples. These are often available at cosmetic counters. Buying before trying is a waste.

Use plain talcum instead of expensive perfumed bath powder.

Stand nearly empty bottles of hand lotion, moisturizer, and other creamy stuff upside down. The cap will accumulate enough to last another week or so.

Learn to cut your kids' hair. Learn well from someone who is good at it. You'll save at least $75 a year per kid.

Don't get sick. Practice preventive health maintenance now. Even with the best insurance, you are going to end up paying for deductibles, copayments, and prescriptions.

Never be without health insurance. High deductibles are fine because you intend to stay healthy. But one catastrophic illness or accident could wipe out everything you have saved and planned for.

Brush and floss daily. Preventive dental care is easy to practice. You can avoid costly gum disease, bridges, and dentures by simply brushing, flossing, and rinsing often.

Keep kids' immunizations up-to-date. Sick kids mean parents must miss work or pay for expensive alternative day care. The costs really add up. Most can be prevented.

Look for free or cheap immunization programs through your local health department.

Make your own flexible ice packs. Pour three-quarters of a cup of water and one-quarter of a cup of rubbing alcohol into a zip-type plastic bag and close it. Put the zipped bag into another bag and seal and freeze it. You will have a slushy bag of ice whenever you need it for sprains, headaches, or whatever.

Shop for health insurance coverage. Often the first-year premium is much less, so changing is not a bad idea. If your employer offers a menu of coverages, check them all carefully. A health-maintenance organization (HMO) might be best for your particular situation.

Always get a second opinion for any major medical procedure. Doctors are human and have been known to make mistakes.

Carefully examine hospital bills. If you go in for a knee reconstruction and are billed for infant nursery time, put up a fuss. Hospitals are notorious for making these kinds of mistakes.

Find a walk-in clinic for emergencies. These twenty-four-hour clinics are popping up all over and are much cheaper than hospital emergency rooms.

Take your own stuff to the hospital. If your doctor approves, you can arrange to take your own food, prescriptions (have the doctor write these out ahead of time so you can pick them up at your discount pharmacy), TV, cellular phone (rent one), and toiletry items. Insist on an à la carte plan so you pay the absolute bare minimum. But be prepared: it's still going to cost a lot to be hospitalized.

If you have to be admitted to a hospital, insist that you go in the day of the surgery. An early admittance will run up your bill and is usually for the convenience of the staff, not the patient.

Inquire about specific hospital fees before you are admitted. Fees do vary considerably from one hospital to the next. Why pay for the availability of kidney machines and heart-transplant teams if you are having knee reconstruction?

Ask questions. Seventy-five percent of all antibiotics taken each year are unnecessary. Doctors know that patients who take the time and trouble to make an office visit expect to be "rewarded" with a prescription! They like to keep their patients happy. Ask the prescribing doctor exactly what the prescription can and cannot do for you and if it is necessary for full recovery.

Always consider generic. Ask your doctor to prescribe the cheapest form of medicine.

Shop for prescriptions. I have found that pharmacies will quote prices over the phone. Call around. You won't believe how the prices vary.

Ask your doctor for free samples. Pharmaceutical companies flood doctors with samples of all kinds of expensive prescriptions. If your doctor doesn't offer, ask.

Buy routine prescriptions through the mail. Many mail-order pharmacies fill prescriptions on a forty-eight-hour basis.

Keep track of parking fees and mileage associated with medical care for tax purposes.

Make a cheap and effective facial mask with milk of magnesia.

Mix baking soda with a little water to get a great facial scrub.

Spritz feet and the inside of shoes with rubbing alcohol in a spray bottle. It's very refreshing and eliminates foot odor.

Soak your fingertips in a fifty-fifty mixture of warm water and white vinegar before applying nail polish. It will last much longer.

Try applying a wet, black tea bag to a nasty canker sore. The tannin acts as an astringent and will relieve the pain and promote healing.

Prevent canker sores by adding four tablespoons of plain yogurt to your diet each day.

Don't smoke. Even a smoking habit that isn't excessive will cost around $1,000 a year and who-knows-how-much more in additional health care.

Take vitamins. Especially take vitamin C, which has been

proven to help stave off colds and flu, lower cholesterol, decrease arthritis pain, reduce outbreaks of canker sores, and alleviate pre-menstrual syndrome, just to name a few benefits. Staying healthy may eliminate expensive doctor visits.

Buy a book on home remedies. Make sure it is written by com-petent doctors and then memorize it! *The Doctor's Book of Home Remedies* (Bantam) is a great one, I've found.

Make your own hot-water bottle. Fill a two-liter plastic soda pop bottle about four inches from the top with hot tap water. Re-place the screw top tightly. Wrap it in a terry cloth towel and snuggle up.

Kids and Families

Don't get divorced. A divorce most certainly will have a dam-aging effect on your finances, to say nothing of your emotions. Just imagine the problem of running two households on what it takes to support one now.

Don't lend money to a friend. It's just too risky to your financial health and your friendship.

Don't lend money to family members. Consider it a gift, and if you just happen to get paid back, it's a bonus.

Open school savings accounts for your kids. Teach them how to fill out deposit slips and make their own deposits. These accounts usually have no minimum balances or service fees.

Share baby-sitting. Work out a plan with your friends to trade favors. Consider starting a baby-sitting co-op. Do research on oth-ers that have been successful.

Teach kids to make lunches. Brown bagging is a good idea—even for Mom and Dad.

Acquaint your family with the local public library. Current newspapers, magazines, children's books, adult books, videos, CDs, wonderful storytelling librarians—what a fabulous place the library is. And it's *free*. If you like to shop for fun, satisfy the impulse by visiting a library. You get to take home something new, and it doesn't cost anything!

Find free entertainment. Family outings do not have to be expensive. Biking, hiking, visiting a park or playground, going on picnics, and attending free concerts are just a few suggestions.

Move to an area with excellent public schools. Save the cost of private-school tuition.

Trade toys. Find a family with kids about the same age as yours. Do a toy swap. "New" toys for free! (Save them up for Christmas and birthdays.) This works best with younger kids.

Take your own snacks to movies and ball games.

Go to a movie matinee. It's always cheaper!

Rent a movie instead of springing for tickets for the entire family.

Don't join record, CD, or book clubs. You can do much better at your local discount stores, and you won't have to worry about sending back selections you don't want.

When buying kids' clothes and shoes, set a budget figure, and if the child wants to upgrade to a trendier brand or style, require her or him to pay the difference.

Perfect reverse psychology. It comes in handy as an effective way of steering adolescents away from expensive tastes.

Dream big. It's free!

Miscellaneous

Plant deciduous trees on the south side of your house. These are trees that lose their leaves in winter. They will provide summer shade without blocking winter sun. Plant evergreens on the north side to shield your home from cold winter winds.

Put cut flowers in the refrigerator when you're at work, asleep, or otherwise unable to enjoy them.

Ask your dry cleaner or neighborhood repair shops to let you know when they have unclaimed goods for sale. There are terrific bargains.

Request a discount whenever you pay cash in a store that honors standard bank credit cards. Since they have to pay from 3 to 7 percent of the bill to the card company on a credit purchase, they should be willing to give you at least part of the difference in the form of a discount. It won't always work, but it's worth a try.

When staying in a hotel, don't make phone calls from your room. Use the pay phone in the lobby and save at least 50 percent, even on your local calls.

Don't carry extra cash. Take along only as much money as you expect to need each day. Impulsive purchases are difficult to make with no dollars to spare.

Think positively. Think about how much you are gaining from your cheapskate lifestyle, not what you are giving up.

Shop for a free checking account. Most banks have them if you ask. There may be certain stipulations, but usually they are quite easy to adhere to. Senior citizens are usually entitled to free accounts without limits.

When entertaining guests for a meal, spend time, not money. The biggest compliment you can pay your dinner guests is to serve dishes that require more preparation than money. Anyone can grill an expensive steak or roast a rack of lamb, but few people make beef bourguignon, lasagna, soufflés, homemade breads, cheesecakes, or other time-consuming dishes, despite how delicious and economical they can be. The hostess who goes to the trouble to prepare such delicacies gives her guests, her family, and her spending plan a treat.

Vacation during the off-season. You can save big-time on everything from travel to hotels and food.

Take up camping. Borrow or rent the gear.

Attend free concerts. Most cities have community-sponsored entertainment during summer months. Many churches and colleges have free performances during holidays.

Work hard. Be a good employee and give a full day's work for a full day's pay. Keep your job.

Be content with what you have. As much as possible, do not spend your life scheming and planning to get more things.

Never buy checks through your bank. You can save more than 50 percent by ordering direct.

Find a bank that doesn't charge a fee for ATM activity. If this is impossible, curb the urge to make many small transactions.

Take it back. If you bought something that you can't use, that you don't like, or that is damaged, for heaven's sake, take it back. Retailers these days are quite anxious to make the customer happy by making adjustments or giving credit or cash refunds. Decide what you want and then stand up for yourself.

Have your pet neutered. Nursing, feeding, and finding homes for litters are costly, both emotionally and financially.

Collect loose change. Make it a habit to dump your pockets and purses every night into one collection receptacle. You won't miss the change, and you'll be amazed how much you can save.

Convince yourself that debt *is a four-letter word.* As soon as you teach that to yourself, teach it to your children. Banish it from your life. (Debt here is understood to be unsecured consumer credit.)

Replace an item only if you cannot get along without it and cannot refurbish, repair, or redo it.

Barter. Whenever possible, trade goods or services instead of money: haircuts for typing, baby-sitting for landscape maintenance, housecleaning for electrical work, etc.

Do not carry credit cards. If you have to own them, keep them in a safe, out-of-the-way place.

Think about a purchase for thirty days before you sign. Any purchase that requires your signature probably requires payments. You just might have a change of heart. If not, then you probably will avoid buyer's remorse and feel confident in your decision.

12

IT'S NEVER TOO LATE

Begin Turning Things Around Today

I received the following letter a while ago, and every time I read it, I'm struck by the sense of desperation it conveys:

> *I've never written or told a living soul of our predicament as I am embarrassed. At our age, most retirees are living comfortably on their assets. But we are not. We are in our seventies and eighties and live on our Social Security and a small pension. We live from one month to the next, and it is a struggle. We always hoped to start saving someday. We need to see if we can better ourselves, but I think it's too late.*
>
> *Yes, we do have credit cards—six of them representing about $4,000 in debt. Our bills get paid on time, because even if we have to take it out of our grocery allowance, they get paid first.*
>
> *Our debt may not seem large to some, but at our age it*

seems like millions. Neither of us can work anymore, so we feel
trapped.

—Betty

The good news for this couple—and everyone—is that it's never too late to become what you want to be. No matter in which season of life you find yourself, it is not too late to get started with your own Money Makeover. It's never too late to start saving, to become filled with the spirit of generosity, or to make necessary adjustments to rein in your spending.

It's not too late to begin listening carefully to the quietest stirrings of your heart. It's not too late to start fulfilling your dreams. Becoming who you want to be may entail a giant leap of faith. It may mean believing that you can hang up a shingle and make a living by following your dreams. It may mean casting yourself as the hero of your own story.

I allowed my eyes to get me into a lot of financial trouble. I saw nice things, and I wanted them. I wanted others to see me as prosperous and well-to-do. I didn't practice restraint, and I did everything I could to have things right now. The rest is history.

I was so busy amassing what I could see that I completely ignored the things I couldn't. My failure to see the invisible was my undoing. I didn't see the miracle of compounded interest—I didn't see what it was doing to me as my foe or what it could have done for me had I embraced it as a friend. I didn't see the underlying problems that drove my irresponsible spending habits. I failed to see the joy and happiness I was stealing from my future.

But it was not too late. I realized that unless I changed the direction I was going in, I would surely end up where I was headed—in deeper and deeper trouble. I turned around. And you can too.

As you begin the rest of your life with your new Money Makeover, look for the invisible. Embrace joy, choose happiness, and hold fast to the intangibles that cannot be taken from you.

Don't become a compulsive hoarder or a compulsive spender. Save, give, plan, anticipate, and then live life to its fullest!

And please, don't deny yourself the simple pleasures in life. Just make sure that if they have a price tag, you pay for them with cash!

Appendix A: The Best of *Cheapskate Monthly* Articles

It's More than Hunting for Bargains

Some people just don't get it. They have no idea what following the *Cheapskate* way of life really means.

Take the radio talk-show host in Charlotte, North Carolina, who recently introduced me as "the country's foremost bargain-hunter. Here she is, ladies and gentlemen . . . the Shopping Queen!"

Or how about the television producers who set up wacky demonstrations to show the world just how cheap I am—gags like separating rolls of two-ply toilet tissue to get twice the amount, collecting and straightening bent nails, and mailing utility payments without postage. Stupid tricks, for sure—entertaining, perhaps—but a far cry from what I'm about and what you're about, too, if you follow the *Cheapskate* philosophy.

The people I find to be most challenged when it comes to

getting it are those who are momentarily speechless when they learn that I don't clip coupons, don't clothe my family at garage sales, and do not believe that buying things on sale is a great way to save money.

Got your attention, huh?

Let me remind you that bargain hunting contributed greatly to landing me into more than $100,000 in unsecured debt. I taught myself how to see anything I really wanted as a bargain. That's all I needed to give myself the green light to purchase. "It's such a good deal, I'll take three!"

I'm trying to forget the time I made a hasty decision to purchase an above-the-ground, fancy-schmancy seven-thousand-gallon swimming pool. Was it a bargain? Well, of course it was. It said right on the sign that the regular price was $3,900. And lucky me, I could pick up that little number for a mere $1,995. I told myself, *Just think how many needless trips to the river or beach could be avoided by having a fabulous water park right in our own backyard. And everyone knows there's no way to put a price tag on good family fun. Yep, it's a bargain.*

Brace yourself. *Cheapskate Monthly* is not subtitled *The Bargain-Hunter's Field Guide*. As a nation, it appears we have bargain shopping down cold. In less than fifty years, our cash-and-carry society turned into one that in the single month of December 2002 charged more than $3.6 billion on credit cards, 66 percent of which will become consumer debt.

So if the *Cheapskate* philosophy is not about finding great deals, what is it about? Let me put it this way: if you were to place the *Credit-Card Junkies' Guide to Debt* at one end of the spectrum, you'd find *Cheapskate Monthly* at the far extreme.

The *Cheapskate* approach to life is about financial balance, which comes as a result of giving away part of your money, saving part of it, and then learning how to reduce the total outgo so that it ends up being less than your income. For the great majority of Americans, this is a concept so foreign that it nearly takes their breath away. And I'm as serious as a heart attack about it. Give first, save next, and then learn how to live within your means.

It's this principle of living within our means—reducing one's monthly expenses to fit within, say, 80 percent of one's income—that's the big challenge for all of us. It's not easy to go from living on 100 percent (or more!) of one's income to living on much less. So we always look for new and reasonable ways to reduce expenses in every area of our lives. Finding bargains can certainly contribute to this quest to reduce expenses, but that represents only one piece in a much larger puzzle.

The *Cheapskate* philosophy is about getting out of debt—unsecured, killer debt. Nothing will sabotage your efforts to live within your means more quickly than spending your hard-earned income servicing consumer debt. While most debt-ridden consumers have given up on ever finding their way back to solvency, I'm here to tell you that it's possible, and I'm ready, willing, and able to show you the way.

Another goal is finding financial peace, which means gaining the kind of security that comes when money for new tires and a brake job is put away long before the tires wear out or the brakes start to squeal. It's about being prepared for unpredictable, irregular, and unexpected expenses (previously characterized as emergencies).

Those who follow the *Cheapskate* approach acknowledge every person's unique income situation and personal preferences. Your means—the amount of money with which you have to work each month—may not be the same as mine, and your lifestyle may be far grander than mine. You may not be required to go to the extremes to which I must go in order to spend less than I make. And my means may allow for a lifestyle different from someone else's.

What's right for me may not be right for you, and vice versa. But as long as we are committed to incurring no new debt and striving to live within our means by giving, saving, and spending less than we earn, we're getting it!

If you've become accustomed to spending more than you earn, can't get around to saving, and, quite frankly, have never even considered giving, the *Cheapskate* way of life may require a new way of thinking and acting.

Still scratching your head about why buying things on sale is not a great way to save money? When you buy things on sale, you might be spending less, but there's no way you're saving money.

There is a big difference.

Dare to Dream

I've got bad news about the American Dream. I'm pretty sure it's all but dead. I know. You didn't even know it was sick.

Ask anyone what the American Dream is, and without fail the matter of home ownership will be in the answer somewhere. In a recent survey conducted by *Money* magazine, 82.3 percent of those surveyed listed owning a home as the number-one most important element in their American Dream. With interest rates down and home values stabilizing in most areas, home ownership appears to be more available than ever. So how could the dream possibly be anything but alive and well? Glad you asked.

Something seriously changed between 1929, when Bill and Agnes McAulay refused to buy a car until their mortgage was paid in full, and 1994, when Chip and Buffy White bought their first home. Not only are the Whites stretching beyond reason simply to make their monthly payments on time, but they also hold absolutely no hope of living long enough to pay the darned thing off. What changed is our definition of home ownership.

To Bill and Agnes, owning their home meant *owning* their home. To Chip and Buffy, owning their home means *owning a mortgage* on their home. Owning a home used to mean having a paid-in-full note and an unclouded title—and hosting a mortgage-burning party. It meant making significant sacrifices until the larger goal was met. Now it means 360 payments, wondering if and when to refinance, unbelievable amounts of interest, and maybe second (and third?) mortgages. And just when the equity is starting to build a little and the payments become comfortable, home ownership invariably means trading into something bigger and better—picking up a new batch of even larger payments.

Come on! Paying off a home mortgage is something people did in the olden days. It simply doesn't happen anymore. I could count on one hand the number of people I know who truly own their homes—and I'd still have three fingers left over.

With the price of a home averaging somewhere around fifty times what one cost in 1929, we should never expect to pay off a mortgage prior to our death, right? We've pretty much given up that dream as something only our grandparents could possibly achieve.

Well, hang on to your hats, folks, because I say let's take back the dream! Sure, homes in the nineties are terribly expensive, but we really can't use housing costs as an excuse. That's because the average income has increased at a far greater rate than housing prices over the past fifty years. I believe that it is possible to pay off your mortgage early, own your home completely free and clear, and look forward to a truly carefree and debt-free retirement. Now is the time to get started.

1. *Formulate a plan.* Several good books are available to help you design a plan that works for your situation. Two especially helpful books are *A Banker's Secret* by Marc Eisenson (Good Advice Press) and *Live Debt Free* by Ted Carroll (Adams, Inc.). What seems like an impossible stretch right now will become realistic in time, and your reward will be great.

2. *Stick to your plan.* Make the goal of owning your home your highest financial priority. Grab onto your plan like a bulldog and don't let go. Make a chart that clearly visualizes the difference between a prepayment plan and the original plan the lender set up.

3. *Teach your children.* Let them in on your plan. Teach them the value of short-term sacrifice to accomplish long-term goals. Make home ownership something to be respected and sought after. If we intend to revive the American Dream, it's going to have to start in our homes.

4. *Plan a party.* Perhaps you've never even thought about it, but when that last payment is made, the lender really will send you the note and deed of trust stamped PAID IN FULL. Frame the original—burn a photocopy in celebration of your great accomplishment.

For those of you who rent and feel that buying a home might be beyond your reach, here's my challenge: Stretch your imagination! Consider alternatives. Programs are available for first-time buyers. Get creative, like the California gentleman who bought a house with a cosigner (because he couldn't qualify on his own). He promptly found two housemates to help him meet his monthly mortgage. Imagine how much more quickly he could prepay the mortgage if he found a third housemate and increased his monthly payment accordingly.

Start dreaming—and dream big! If you can dream it, chances are good that you can accomplish it. And don't forget to invite me to the mortgage-burning party.

Anatomy of a Supermarket

I never thought much about the logistics and intense marketing genius behind the supermarket business and all of its subliminal aspects until one day, in a tremendous hurry, I dashed into my favorite market only to find it had been completely rearranged the previous night. How dare they mess with my mind! The harder I searched for the items I needed, the more frustrated I became. In my usual timid manner, I went directly to the store manager to register my complaint and was told that this was just business as usual for a profit-conscious, modern-day supermarket. In frustration, I stormed out with only part of what I had intended to purchase.

Later on, when I had regained my composure, I went back and had an enlightening conversation with the manager. It seems that a store of that magnitude has pretty high overhead and allocates a large portion of its advertising budget to finding ways to appeal to customers' compulsive shopping habits.

It has been proven that the typical shopper quickly memorizes the layout of the store, knows exactly where to find the items needed, and becomes oblivious to products not regularly purchased. But by turning the place upside down every year or so, the store can "introduce" its regular shoppers to thousands of products they might never have noticed if the store remained unchanged. And to be ever so much more helpful, the merchandising experts determined that larger shopping carts would be nice. Ever notice how much larger those carts are than they were ten years ago? The experts know that most people shop till the cart's full! I can only imagine what they are planning for the future. Maybe motorized carts complete with rearview mirror, turn signals, and optional trailer—all for the shopper's convenience, of course.

The average food shopper spends over an hour every week in a semicomatose state, shuffling up and down the aisles of the all-American supermarket, snatching item after item, building an expensive tower in a basket. At the end of the exercise, the score is tallied, and in most cases the supermarket is the clear winner. The ordinary shopper is as predictable as a rat following a trail of cheese right into a trap.

The most expensive and frivolous items are usually placed at eye level. Baking staples such as flour and sugar are commonly on low shelves or so high up you have to reach for them. Eye-catching displays with lights, bells, and whistles usually promote junk-type and expensive items, even though they are piled up to appear to be on sale.

The center aisles usually house the prepared and brightly packaged, overprocessed food items. Either a hot deli or a bakery in the store will be emitting heavenly smells to appeal to your senses and start those compulsive buying juices flowing. The perimeter of the store is the safe zone—produce, dairy, and meat.

You probably can't avoid the supermarket completely, and it is difficult to remain completely true to your shopping list and financial plan in these kinds of stores. But you can commit to doing regular shopping in a no-frills warehouse store and enter the supermarket with extreme *caution,* fully aware of the many ways your compulsiveness is being tested.

It's a safe bet that food shopping will be more than an optional pastime for the rest of your life. You have two choices: either lapse into an even deeper comatose state or get smart.

Suffering Employment Insecurity?

It seems that the words *job* and *security* really do not go together anymore. All you need to do is pick up today's newspaper and read which company has just completed another major layoff (the term *downsizing* has become popular, perhaps because it sounds more reasonable than *massive firings*). Here is today's headline in my paper: "GM Loses $4.5 Billion, Cuts to the Bone; Firm to Close Plants, Slash 74,000 Jobs; Workers in Shock."

I don't know about you, but I would much prefer a root canal without anesthesia to a blind-side unemployment hit!

These days unemployment has absolutely no respect. It is hunting down elite executives just the same as clerical and factory workers. Unemployment does not seem to be singling out any one particular part of the country either. Forecasters of employment trends don't seem to be predicting any imminent change in the situation.

So what's the answer? Give in to the three Ws—wish, whine, and worry? Hold a pity party? No, that won't accomplish anything.

Try this analogy: I live in California, where the threat of earthquakes is pretty high. But I still live here voluntarily, and so do a lot of others. Areas of the East Coast live with the seasonal threat of hurricanes. But I don't see those areas becoming unpopulated anytime soon. We have learned to prepare for these disasters. My kids learned "duck and cover" right along with fire drills from the first day of preschool. We have certain disaster plans in place—just in case. New California laws require every employer to have a safety manual in the event someone just happens to accidentally drink copier toner (among other potential emergencies)! My point is that we prepare for the most remote of potential disasters while leaving ourselves completely open to more likely crises.

Wise persons should prepare for unemployment. Tomorrow holds no guarantees. A proactive posture can prevent us from reacting to devastation with shock.

Workplace Trends, a newsletter for management types, says that job security for both blue-collar and white-collar workers was a phenomenon that occurred after World War II and is now history. Today's corporate executive can plan to change employers an average of seven times during his or her career—and not always voluntarily.

So I would like to unveil the Official Cheapskate Employment Disaster Preparedness Plan. Nothing new—just some focused common sense.

Part I. Do Everything Necessary to Stay Employed

1. *Consider your job a blessing.* Obviously this is easier for some than others! If you "think thankfulness" for your employer, you might actually start feeling that way.

2. *Step up your savings program.* Experts say you need the equivalent of three to six months' expenses set aside for possible loss of employment. Impossible, you say? You can do it!

3. *Become an expert on which alternative employment possibilities are available.* Read the "Help Wanted" sections of the classifieds regularly to keep educated.

4. *Start a file on employment alternatives.* Learn what additional requirements you might need should you decide to make a career change.

5. *Update your résumé—just in case.* It's not a bad idea to review and update it every six months.

6. *At the first sign of serious weakness in your industry or firm, step up your job search.* Whatever you do, don't quit one job until you have landed another.

7. *Make your decision to change jobs as unemotionally as possible.* Trade in your nerves for excitement—two closely related emotions.

8. *Weigh your decisions carefully.* Don't avoid making a change just because you feel obligated to go down with a sinking ship.

Part II. In the Event of Unemployment

1. *Don't panic.* Those who love and depend on you need you to stay calm and smart.

2. *Don't pay off your debts with severance pay, stock plans, or any lump sums you might have received upon separation from your employer.* You're going to need those resources for living essentials.

3. *Determine how long you can hold out by using your cash to cover the bare necessities.* This will give you a clear picture of what you need to do.

4. *Make a job-hunting plan.* Network! You never know when Aunt Susie's hairdresser's husband's boss's sister-in-law's nephew might be looking for someone with your exact qualifications.

5. *Keep a positive attitude, even if you have to fake it for a while.*

6. *Consider taking temporary employment provided it is in your field or profession.*

7. *Remember: everything is going to be okay!*

Sleepless in Southern California

In the middle of the night last Tuesday, I was lying awake thinking about mail. I get a lot of it. Mail doesn't usually cause insomnia for me, but this particular night it did. Not all of the mail, just one letter sincerely handwritten on yellow, lined paper and signed by a faithful reader.

Dear Mary,

I am writing in response to a letter you published in the November 1993 issue of Cheapskate Monthly. *I am, in fact, very angry because the letter does not belong in your newsletter.*

A woman wrote and said she decided to try your methods for saving money and paying off her credit cards. In three months, she has managed to save $2,500, and in four months, she will have paid off four of her seven credit cards.

Anyone who can save $200 a week does not have financial problems. Not only can she save over $800 a month, but she can even pay off four credit cards within four months. This woman is apparently rich. Please write stories about people who really have to change their lifestyles once they stop charging. It takes much sacrifice to try to pay for things with cash only, apply money to credit-card bills, and also try to save a tiny bit, too! I felt I couldn't let this bother me any longer so I just had to write.

Sign me, Discouraged.

I just couldn't sleep until I answered.

Dear Discouraged,

I believe you have missed the entire focus of this newsletter. It has nothing to do with "rich" or "poor." It's about learning to live within one's income, regardless of what amount of money that might be. Cheapskate Monthly *readers range from single parents struggling to survive at near-poverty levels to professionals making six figures per year . . . and more.*

You might find it difficult to believe that within this newsletter's family there are members who make huge incomes, but because they have never learned to apply principles of financial responsibility in order to control their spending, they are in terrible situations. They pay huge amounts of interest, struggle to pay the bills, fork over staggering late fees, and dodge creditors. Their problems are no different from yours—just a lot bigger.

I'm afraid you believe the myth that all your financial problems would immediately cease if you just had more money, if you were "rich."

The truth is that unless one learns to live according to principles of financial responsibility—which include consistent saving, generous giving, and bringing expenses in line with income—more money will just make one's current problems greater. It won't solve them.

Unfortunately, increasing one's income is the qualifier for more debt. That seems to have become the American way. Many people see an extra $500 a month as a way to get that new car or refurbish the house or handle a larger house payment.

Although most of us have great intentions of paying off bills with the additional income, the tax-refund check, or the relief promised by a debt-consolidation loan, unless old habits are replaced with new ones, the same debting patterns will return. Eventually the original problem of not enough money will return on a much larger scale. The new and bigger problems will require even more money. Believe me, anyone can outspend their income. Greater income does not automatically insure financial responsibility.

I know nothing more about the California letter writer than what we both learned from her letter. Her excitement leads me to believe that saving and repaying debt are something new for her. Why else would she be so anxious to share her joy? Her new behaviors having to do with saving and repaying debt are nothing short of remarkable, as are yours.

The progress she is experiencing in handling her finances is what Cheapskate Monthly *is all about! It is possible that the $200 a week she's been able to save is far below her eventual goal of saving 10 percent of everything she earns. Her struggles in that area are probably no different from your own. None of us knows just what changes and sacrifices she and her family have had to make in order to bring some sanity to their finances.*

The purpose of Cheapskate Monthly *is to help those who are struggling to live within their means to find practical and realistic methods and solutions to their financial problems. If you don't think high-income individuals can have financial problems, you need to meet Donald Trump or Carl Karcher or any number of your fellow* Cheapskate Monthly *subscribers.*

For the life of me I can't come up with one reason that would preclude that encouraging letter from appearing in this publication. I have a feeling she could probably teach all of us something about discipline and determination.

I hope that you will reconsider your reaction to the letter. To be able to rejoice in another's success could be a growing experience for you. When a member of our family experiences success, I believe cartwheels are in order.

—Mary

Think Sacrifice, Not Deprivation

Every year, some national poll publishes the Top Ten New Year's Resolutions. Invariably number one goes something like this: "I'm going to get my finances in order." I'm not surprised, are you?

Considering that Americans are deeper in debt than ever, bankruptcy filings are at an all-time high, and personal savings are embarrassingly low, I can only assume the obvious: year after year the most popular resolution is dumped until the next New Year. Budgets, diets, and New Year's resolutions must top the list of Things Most Likely to Fail. I think I know why. Each of them spells *deprivation*. Deprivation feels terrible, and we can handle it for only short periods of time before we simply cave in and give up.

I can't help but recall the times I attempted to stop using my credit cards. And I really tried to stop writing checks when there was no money to back them up. The problem was that cutting myself off from my ability to spend felt like ripping away a part of myself—as if I were losing my security, comfort, and status in life. I felt like I was being punished and deprived of what I loved the same way a prisoner is deprived of freedom and personal choice.

Again and again I tried to reform, but the feelings of loss and the fear of deprivation were much stronger than any desire to change. A battle was raging inside of me, and I controlled neither side. Instead, I was controlled by overwhelming feelings and out-of-control desires.

The irony is that in doing so many crazy things to make sure I never felt deprived, I was paving the way for the ultimate deprivation—the total loss of everything in my life that truly mattered. I get chills recalling just how close we came to total financial disaster.

I've come to realize that the whole subject of reforming one's financial situation has two distinct aspects: *economics* and *emotions*. If you have tried to cure your money ills only to fail, it's likely you were dealing only with the economics. Both sides demand equal attention.

I've found dealing with the economic side of personal finances to be fairly simple because it is so straightforward. It's math. It's adding and subtracting. It's agreeing that I cannot spend more money than I have and finding ways to spend less and keep more. When it comes to the economics of personal money management, there are right and wrong answers, black and white issues. And they're readily available in thousands of budget books on the shelves of libraries, bookstores, and homes of this country.

Then there's the emotional aspect of financial change, the part most ignored and least dealt with. Dealing with our emotions is much more difficult than handling the economics, because emotions are subjective. We see their result, but we don't understand them. We can't put them on a spreadsheet and move them around until they balance perfectly. We can't project them the way we project income and expenses.

I struggled because my emotions were so powerful that they overcame all economic good sense and rendered any potential change completely out of the question. That's until I discovered I *can* control my emotions. I cannot pretend they don't exist, but I don't have to be victimized by them either.

Somewhere along the line in my journey to solvency, I made a profound, life-changing discovery. I learned that I could replace my fear of deprivation with the joy of sacrifice. I learned to harness my powerful emotions, turning them into my ally instead of my enemy. I purposely set out to embrace sacrifice and reject all feelings of deprivation.

Sacrifice means to give up something of value for the sake of something else that is more important or worthier. Deprivation means to have a possession or enjoyment taken away. Sacrifice focuses on a goal. Deprivation focuses on poor me. Once I learned the startling difference between the two concepts, I understood why meaningful change kept eluding me.

The practice of sacrifice in the context of changing one's financial condition is a kind of art form that is improved with practice. First, you must identify your worthier goal. Without a purpose, your sacrifice will indeed be nothing more than deprivation. You need a worthy cause on which to focus.

Perhaps your worthy cause is to get out of debt once and for all, or take a once-in-a-lifetime family vacation. Maybe you want to allocate more money to give to your church. Or maybe your noble purpose is to save and invest money for your retirement.

Let's say, for example, that you're committed to being debt-free three years from now and to that end you are willing to make the necessary sacrifices. Just saying you're going to be debt-free is nice, but you need more than that. You need a written and measurable plan. You need a specific strategy that outlines exactly how you are going to reach your goal. You'll need to establish benchmarks so that you can measure your progress and look back to see how far you've come.

Focusing on the worthy cause and visualizing its importance and value are the way to combine the economic and emotional sides of financial change. Living each day with the goal in mind and practicing how you'll feel when that final debt is wiped out are the ways to control your emotions.

I'm not suggesting that sacrifice won't be painful at times. The changes you will be required to make will be difficult. But when you focus on the worthier goal, sacrifice becomes tolerable. With practice you will see the connection between a small sacrifice and the great reward.

If you've decided to make the journey to meaningful financial change, you're going to need lots of encouragement and understanding from your fellow travelers. We all need those because we are emotional beings—we thrive on approval and validation. We need empathy from those who understand what we're going through when the path gets steep and rocky.

As we make progress and reach our goals, we need encouragement to keep going so that we can continue reaching for the next goal, and the next, and the next. Find people in your life who can offer that kind of support and reassurance.

These Friends of Mine

The following article was written in response to a letter I received from a frustrated subscriber, who wished to be known as "Bob."

Once upon a time, on the outskirts of a village nestled in a beautiful kingdom, there lived a young man named Bob, his wife, Sue, and their young son, Bobby.

One day Bob, having just entered the fourth decade of life, gathered his little family around him and exclaimed excitedly, "We're right on target in building our future. We've paid off our debts (except for our mortgage), we have this lovely little cottage, and we've saved and invested so well we now have $70,000 working hard for us. We have saved for Bobby's education and are well prepared to withstand the storms of life. We have a bright future. If we keep this up, we will be able to live in our dream palace by the time we reach the prime of our lives."

By and by, Bob and Sue became friends with others in their village. As their friendships grew, so did Bob's curiosity. Being lured to the bright lights of the other side of the village, he said to himself, How in the world are these newfound friends of ours, who are of equally common heritage, able to afford such magnificent palaces complete with opulent furnishings, luxurious automobiles, and domestic staffs?

"How can this be?" Bob asked them courageously. "It's no secret we all have about the same income. How is it that I can afford but a small cottage for my family while you live in such luxury? How can I, too, provide so well for my family and impress others in the village the way you have impressed me?"

"It is easy," said one of Bob's friends. "Do as we do. First you must give up your silly notions about saving for the future. You must agree to spend every dollar you earn plus every dollar you hope to earn in the future. Next, go to the town square and gather about yourself plastic of every color. You will find a different piece of plastic in every shop. Soon new pieces of plastic will come to you automatically without request or inquiry. With all of your plastic, you must race out into the highways and byways and acquire everything you want."

Another friend chimed in, "Don't forget an Olympic-style pool like ours in which to exercise your lean, young bodies. In this way you will surely provide happiness for your family. We will even show you clever tricks like how to use your new plastic to make payments on your old plastic. Above all, you must eat, drink, and debt today, for tomorrow you may die!"

Terribly perplexed and feeling tempted to join his friends in their affluence so he could enjoy life to its fullest, Bob asked for an audience before the wisest old woman (meaning nothing more than that she was slightly older than he) in all the kingdom.

"Oh, Wise Old Woman," said Bob. "For all these years, I've done the right thing. I've saved as you taught me, and my money has grown little by little through the miracle of compounding interest. I've carried a brown bag and gone without pocket money. I've planned all my spending. We've dined on sumptuous fare in the fine restaurants of the kingdom only when I could pay with cash. I've waited to purchase quality furniture for our small cottage until the proper amount of money was saved and the best deal found.

"My wife and young son do not complain," Bob continued. "It is I, Wise Old Woman, who see the palaces in the village. I salivate over the beautiful vehicles that make my paid-for cart look sad. I am embarrassed. I want those beautiful things for my family, and I want them now. What good is it to build for the future when I may not live to see it? My friends say I should live for today, for by the time I reach middle age, I may be dead and gone. And then what good will all my planning have been?

"These friends of mine encourage me to gather about myself plastic of every color and with it acquire a whopper of a palace and all the furnishings and vehicles my heart could ever desire. They promise me that only then will I find true happiness. If they are right and these things truly hold the secret to happiness, I am missing out by building for my future instead of living high on the hog as they do.

"Please, Wise Old Woman. Is life really passing me by, as my friends insist? Am I doing the right thing, or is it my friends who are really right? Please reassure me before I haul off and do something stupid."

The Wise Old Woman, who had listened intently, responded gently and knowingly, almost as if she'd been one of these friends in another place, another time.

"Your friends mean well, my dear Bob, but they are nuts. They are walking a high wire while juggling very heavy debts.

They have no safety net. With arrogance they look to the future demanding they be granted health and employment to some-day pay for all of the things they so foolishly feel they must have today.

"They are putting their marriages at risk with unthinkable pressure caused by the weight of the heavy debts. They are young and strong right now, but in time they will become weak and unable to keep up the juggling. They will crash unless they take immediate steps to come down from the high life and learn to live according to the wise principles you have learned. If they do not change their ways, they will in time surely be bankrupt.

"What your friends say is true: Life is uncertain. Perhaps you will be dead before you reach middle age. But chances are far greater, my son, that you will not die young and you will live to be ninety or even one hundred. Likewise your friends will live long lives and will face great sorrow as the foolishness of their youth destroys the joy of their old age.

"Do not envy them, young Bob. Instead, pity them for the peril that lies ahead. Befriend them and be there to comfort them when the pain of crashing threatens to destroy them. Re-frain from saying, 'I told you so!' for indeed they will be in such misery, it will not be necessary. They will know.

"Continue living according to those wise financial princi-ples that have brought you this far and have given you such a firm foundation. Do not allow your emotions to determine your attitudes. Your emotions cannot be trusted. They are fickle and change like the wind. Instead, work hard, give generously, save well, spend wisely."

With that the Wise Old Woman stood and reached out her hands to Bob and said, "You will now be highly revered in the land and shall from this day forward be known as the second-wisest person in all the kingdom. Wear your banner proudly, for truly you are an example to which all the inhabitants of the kingdom aspire."

Feeling a sense of renewal and purpose, Bob ran home to the small cottage on the outskirts of the village nestled in the beautiful kingdom. As he burst into the small cottage, he gathered up his wife and young son and pledged to never again envy those walking the high wire and juggling heavy debts.

"I've learned the truth this day," he exclaimed. "We will be patient to grow rich slowly and prepare well for our future. We will find contentment not in what we have but in who we are. I will provide for you, my little family. I will work hard, give generously, save well, and look forward to our bright future."

And so it was that Bob, Sue, and little Bobby from that day forward began to live happily ever after.

About a year after publishing this story in *Cheapskate Monthly*, I heard again from our friend "Bob." Much had transpired in that year, including the addition of a baby girl to his family:

Hey, Mary, it's me, Bob, the guy who lives "on the outskirts of the village nestled in a beautiful kingdom." I wrote to you last year because I was envious of my friends' luxurious lifestyles. But no more! The tables turned, and now the friends who once made fun of me for being tight admit my style of life makes a lot of sense. Like many of your readers, my wife and I have worked our way out of all debt except for our mortgage. I must admit your suggestion that we also pay that debt off struck me as a nice thought but more likely a pipe dream.

Not long ago, our mortgage holder substituted detailed monthly mortgage statements for the old payment coupons. What a revelation! When I looked at the first statement, my mouth fell open. In the three years since refinancing our home, we paid only the closing costs and not one penny of principal. That simple examination started me thinking in new ways about our all-American, thirty-year mortgage. A few quick calculations revealed that in thirty years we will end up paying for our house almost three times over! If we continue as we have, we'll pay $300,000 for our $100,000 home. But the real kicker is that I will have to make more than $500,000 to come up with the $300,000, allowing for taxes and tithes.

Have we gone completely nuts?! Considering that most people move every five years or so, and mortgages are set up so that little is paid toward the principal during those first years, millions of us are doomed to pay mostly interest for the rest of our lives. It's like throwing money in the trash. The average person will likely earn between $1 and $2 million in his or her working lifetime—and still end up broke. Between mortgage interest, auto-financing interest, credit-card interest, and taxes, over half of all the money the average person earns could go for nothing. I for one have had it with throwing my money away on interest.

Here we are, a couple that uses coupons religiously and closely watches every expense. I take a brown-bag lunch to work, we eat out one night a week, and we buy clothes during clearance sales. We wouldn't dream of going to a full-price movie, yet we're giving away hundreds of dollars every month to the mortgage company. Hundreds!

Our credit-crazy, monthly-payment, brainwashed society never talks about paying off a mortgage early. Such an undertaking is thought to be not only impossible but unthinkable! We live in a society that doesn't want us to pay off our bills. It wants us to be constantly borrowing and paying interest.

Like millions of our peers, we've been making our house

payments each month, and up until now assumed there was little we could do but ride it out to the bitter end. But the thought was just too depressing, so I kept figuring and searching for a better way. We've decided to apply every available dollar to our mortgage, including the 10 percent we save. I've worked on this idea from every angle, and the result is clear—if we stick to our plan, we will own our home free and clear in less than five years.

We will not sell our investments or touch our accumulated savings, but we'll stop funding them on a regular basis as we have been. We are now redirecting everything to prepaying the mortgage—the regular house payment, what we would be paying for a car, what we'd normally be putting into savings. In other words, all money not spent on living expenses and any extra funds that come along. Seeing that loan balance fall every month is the best feeling in the world. God willing, my wife and I will be thirty-eight years old with no house payment five years from now.

When the house is paid in full, we'll resume investing 10 percent and put all the house-payment funds into a Next-House Account. When we decide to move up, we can pay cash or assume a small mortgage that we'll pay down the same way. We definitely see a larger, more beautiful home in our future, and feel this is the best way we can fulfill that dream.

—Bob

And my reply:

I think you have a fabulous plan! And I like your style—it's aggressive, no-nonsense, and determined. Interest is always a killer, but there's nothing like seeing the facts and figures of a thirty-year mortgage on paper to get one's attention. You've discovered the secret the banking industry would just as soon you never find out: advance payments stop the bank or mortgage holder from collecting compound interest on the amount you prepay—not just once, but month after month, year after year.

Since you have already accumulated savings and other investments, I think you are doing the wise thing by "investing" everything you can into your mortgage. That's exactly what you are doing when you apply your savings to that outstanding debt.

Mortgage prepayment represents a low-risk investment, and the rate of return is guaranteed because making early principal payments will save you the interest payments you have agreed to make. It's a smart thing for someone in your situation to do.

However, I wouldn't recommend such an aggressive plan to the family carrying credit-card debts or one with little or no savings. These folks need to first pay off those debts and work on accumulating savings equal to several months' expenses in case of a job loss or sudden illness. Nor would I recommend aggressive prepayment if one's home were showing a steady decline in value.

Well, my dear Bob, you've certainly lived up to your designation as the "second-wisest person in all the kingdom," and I have a distinct feeling you've made the Wise Old Woman very proud.

P.S. Maybe we shouldn't be too rough on the all-American, thirty-year mortgage. After all, without that financing vehicle, few of us would ever be able to purchase a home. Such a mortgage might be the very thing that makes it possible for you to own your dream house completely free and clear someday soon! The key is to use the thirty-year loan to acquire the property and then pay it back as quickly as possible.

But First Consider the Consequences

I wish I had a quarter for every stupid purchase I've made in my life. I'd have some major coinage. Regrettably, my financial faux pas have been remarkable in both quantity and quality. I've made some real doozies.

Take the aboveground swimming pool. Its à la carte price was bad enough. Adding everything required but not included took it past barely reasonable to absolutely ridiculous. First there were the heater and filter. Then a cover, chemicals, and test kit. Of course, we needed search-and-rescue equipment (this was one monstrosity of a pool) and a few necessary pool toys. Oh, and let's not forget the cost of eventually getting rid of the albatross. Let me put it this way: There is not a lively secondary market for this kind of thing.

If I'd had the courage to consider the consequences of such a major purchase before making the decision to buy, I am quite certain we could have avoided a five-year industrial-strength headache and saved one huge pile of dough.

I've since learned how important it is to keep a simple self-test handy. A checklist clears away impulsivity and allows good sense to prevail.

This process allows for no feelings-based answers. Nothing that includes "I feel" or words like *happy, disappointed, sad, guilty, or afraid*. This exercise is about facts, not feelings. Feelings are fickle. They trick us, but, worse, they change like the wind. When it comes to making wise financial decisions, feelings cannot be trusted.

Do I need it? If the honest answer is no and you do not have oodles of discretionary income, case closed. You've just saved yourself from a foolish purchase.

Can I afford it? If you have to go into debt to make the purchase, you cannot afford it. Forget it.

Do I already have something that will do just as well? An honest assessment of all the stuff you already have could easily produce an affirmative answer to this question. End of discussion.

Can I wait until I find a cheaper, more reasonable substitute? Have you ever noticed that you require your children to be patient but rarely put the same requirement on yourself? The bonus with this question is that while you are waiting, the need often disappears.

Have I found the best deal? It takes time and effort to comparison shop, and that also makes for breathing room. When making wise decisions, time is a valuable ingredient.

Am I willing to wait? A false sense of urgency brought on by overwhelming desire—or a sale—can really skew your otherwise good sense. Simply getting away from the situation for a couple of days has a remarkable way of clearing your mind. If the purchase is right for you today, it will still be right a few days from now.

What if I don't? Make a list of things that will happen if you don't make the transaction. If it's paying the rent you're questioning, that's simple. The consequence is eviction. You must proceed. But if the subject is buying another pair of shoes, a faster computer, or season tickets to the symphony, the consequences of not making the purchase will be quite different.

What if I do? Here's where the rubber meets the road. What will be the exact consequences of going through with this transaction? Don't cheat on yourself. Don't accept "I don't know" as an answer. If you don't know the true costs, you are not ready to make the decision.

So you think my pool fiasco was a financial disaster? Truth be told, that purchase were small compared to impulsive acquisitions I've considered since then. Trust me. And no one is more grateful than I—my husband being a close second—that I've learned to consider the consequences first.

Eight Words to Change Your Life

You hear it all the time, but do you know what it means to live below your means? More importantly, have you figured out how to do that?

To live below your means is to create a lifestyle you can pay for with money left over. Living below your means in this high-pressure, credit-based, gotta-have-it-all-right-now society is not exactly easy. It takes skill and determination to go against the tide and buck a system that encourages spending all we have now plus what we hope we'll get in the future.

Here's the secret for living below your means: *buy what you need, want what you have.* That's it. Eight words that could change your life forever. Eight words that point the way to contentment.

Have you ever considered that contentment is every credit-card company's worst nightmare? It's no secret that they spend bazillions of dollars every year on marketing and ad campaigns to create discontentment and dissatisfaction because these translate into huge profits. They want us to believe we cannot be happy without the stuff they say we deserve even if we cannot pay for it now. From the looks of things, their efforts are succeeding quite well.

Advertising has become such a part of our culture that we are mostly unaware of the ways it influences our desires, the ways we spend our money, and to what extent we're willing to legally obligate money we've not yet earned.

A while back, I read in the *New York Times* that the average American adult is the target of some thirty-five hundred commercial ads in a single day. How outrageous is that? Sure, we live in a highly commercialized society—but thirty-five hundred ads? In a single day? I figured that had to be a gross exaggeration.

I decided to conduct my own test. I would count the ads I heard or saw in my typical day. I knew it wouldn't come anywhere close to thirty-five hundred.

The next morning the radio alarm sounded, and before I could even open my eyes, I needed to put two hash marks on my score pad. So prolific were the ads on television I could barely keep an accurate count and get ready at the same time.

Of course, I had to count every message, banner, business placard, real-estate sign, billboard, license-plate frame, bumper sticker, commercial vehicle, and bus I saw on the way to work, all the while being careful not to miss any radio ads. Good thing I wasn't driving.

Reading the newspaper boosted my count significantly, as did flipping through a few magazines. Have you ever counted the ads in a typical woman's magazine? Try it sometime.

Logging onto the Internet shot my count through the roof. The mail arrived at 10:00 A.M., and that's when I surrendered. Not only was it impossible to get anything done while counting the commercial influences on my fairly low-key, ho-hum kind of a day, but I couldn't keep up with the pace. It was a mind-boggling exercise.

Thirty-five hundred ads per adult per day? Easy! Needless to say, I became a believer.

So how can we practice contentment, embrace the eight words, and in so doing counteract commercial influences that attempt to sabotage our efforts to live below our means?

INSULATE. When with genuine gratitude you choose to want what you have, you build a layer of insulation around your life that will protect you from the harshness of overcommercialization. Reading the fine print, analyzing what clearly is too good to be true, and questioning outrageous commercial messages are also good ways to increase that protective insulation.

ISOLATE. If you are easily dissatisfied or prone to impulsive behaviors, identify your weak spots, then isolate yourself from them. Turn off the television. Skip past the magazine ads. Ban the use of vending machines. Isolate yourself from mindless shopping. Throw mail-order catalogs in the trash unopened (and I mean the smelly trash so you won't be tempted to retrieve them). Put distance between you and places where you are most likely to slip back into your old ways of spending beyond your means.

SELF-TALK. Confronting yourself is a great way to build your strength against the strong current of commercialization. Ask yourself these kinds of questions and then expect honest answers:

- Do I need this?
- Don't I have something already that will do just as well?
- Am I sure this is a good value?
- Do I have the cash to pay for it?
- Could I delay the purchase for a few weeks?
- Am I willing to sit on my decision for twenty-four hours before acting?

Never feel you must apologize for choosing the high road when it comes to managing well the money that flows into your life.

Living below your means is a way to build wealth, reduce stress, create options, and find peace of mind.

Living below your means is an honorable way to conduct your life.

The Power of a Grateful Heart

In the aftermath of the most heinous atrocity ever committed on American soil, Americans did an amazing thing: they reached out and gave.

The common thread through all of the amazing outpouring in response to September 11 has been that, in spite of it all, we have so much for which to be grateful. Giving is the way we express that profound gratitude.

Gratitude is more than an annual ritual performed hastily before diving into the Thanksgiving meal. It's more than a holiday decoration and more than a snappy word that rhymes with "attitude." Of all the human emotions, gratitude is the most powerful. It is so powerful it can obliterate fear, hopelessness, and doubt. Gratitude can heal a broken heart, slow the aging process, and restore broken relationships. Gratitude creates hope, and hope brings joy. It is in joy, not fear, that we find strength.

Greed Is the Enemy

Never before in the history of our country has so much meant so little to so many. The easy availability of credit, which allows us a way to live beyond our means, has enabled greed to creep into every area of our lives. Some call the affliction *affluenza*: an unhappy condition of overload, debt, anxiety, and waste resulting from the dogged pursuit of more. The more we have, the more we want. The more we want, the more it takes to feel satisfied. The more credit we accept, the further into debt we slip. The more we have, the greedier we become and the more we suffer from possession overload. We let what we lack eclipse any feelings of gratitude for what we already have.

Affluenza in its advanced stages leads to stress. And stress leads to the breakdown of mental and physical health. Gratitude is the antidote.

Gratitude, the conscious and heartfelt expression of appreciation and thankfulness, is the number-one best antidote for dissatisfaction. Greed says, "I must have more"; gratitude counters with, "I have more than enough." Greed says, "My life is pathetic"; gratitude says, "I am so blessed." Greed steals joy; gratitude restores it.

To develop gratitude requires that you talk to yourself and regularly write down your thoughts. The idea is to begin to see all of life, even the difficult times, as challenges, opportunities, and blessings. You may also find it helpful to reframe a situation—to choose to see it from a new perspective.

Reframing can be difficult, but especially important, when misfortune strikes. If you wreck your car, that is unfortunate. Still, if you are aware that you wrecked your car, that is something for which to be grateful, because it means you're alive. And it's bonus blessings if no one was hurt, you have a good insurance policy, or the car wasn't totaled.

Authentic and heartfelt gratitude can "hush up" insatiable desires and negative attitudes. For instance, you can hate your job, hate the boss, hate the people, hate the commute, and hate the work. Or you can be genuinely grateful that you have a job today. You can learn to appreciate everything about that job, even the distasteful aspects, because they build your character, your tolerance, and compassion. No matter what the situation, you choose your focus. If you choose fear and anger, expect depression and misery. If you choose to respond with a grateful heart, expect hope, satisfaction, and joy. Yes, joy even in the midst of adversity.

Giving Is the Action

Want to pull the plug on your greed? Become a giver. Giving away some of what is precious to you—yes, your money—is the ultimate thank-you note. Giving opens the door to God's blessings and our eyes to the big picture. It allows us to see the world through new eyes of compassion. Giving is an outward expression of a personal affirmation that no matter how bleak your situation may appear, you really do have enough.

A Risk-Free, High-Yield, Guaranteed Investment

Now and then someone asks me a question more or less like this: "How can I get started investing in stocks and mutual funds that are risk-free and have guaranteed high rates of return?"

Of course, that makes me laugh hysterically, not only because such things don't exist, but even more because someone thinks I am an investment adviser.

I am simply not qualified to advise anyone on traditional Wall Street stock-market investing. My investment advice is quite un-conventional, but it makes so much sense you are going to be amazed.

Why Invest?

Why do we all have such a desire to invest? So we can read pro-spectuses and attend shareholder meetings? Not likely. We want our money to grow; we want to build wealth. We want to increase our net worth.

Net worth simply means that dollar figure that represents the financial value of everything you own (assets) less everything you owe (liabilities). If you owe more than you own, you have a negative net worth.

Increase Net Worth

You can increase your net worth in two ways—increase your assets or decrease your liabilities. If you agree that the reason you want to invest is to increase your personal net worth, I have good news for you. There may be an easier and a better way to do that than to plunge yourself into the stock market, where the risk may exceed your comfort level.

INCREASE ASSETS Here's an example. Say you do have money invested in the stock market. That counts as an asset, and if it increases in value, that will have a positive affect on your net worth—it too will increase. That's the same as building your wealth. But since there are no guarantees and all stock-market investments are at risk, it's possible things will go the other way. If the value of your asset decreases, so will your net worth.

DECREASE LIABILITIES All the amounts you owe on credit cards, mortgages, student loans, and car loans are your liabilities. Each dollar you owe decreases your net worth. And conversely, every dollar you pay back reduces your total liability and therefore increases your net worth. Paying back debt is a very reasonable way to increase your net worth.

There Is No Difference

If you have debt, your net worth will increase at the very same rate if you increase your assets or decrease your liabilities. Let's say you receive a $1,000 bonus with which you buy shares in a mutual fund. Your net worth increases by $1,000. If instead you repay $1,000 of debt, your net worth still increases by $1,000.

Invest in Your Debt

RISK-FREE. Using the example above, let's say you bought the Home Depot stock instead of paying off $1,000 of debt. Next month the stock takes a nosedive and drops by 50 percent. Now your stock is worth $500. But if you pay off debt with that $1,000 and the Home Depot stock tanks, it does not affect your net worth at all. That $1,000 "investment" in your debt increased your net worth without any risk. That's a high rate of return. Investing in your debt pays you interest equal to the amount of the interest you were paying on the debt.

Go back to the $1,000 debt you paid off in the previous example. If it was a credit-card balance at, say, 18 percent interest, you were paying $15 in interest each month or $180 annually on that debt if you were making only minimum payments each month. Once you pay it off, you no longer have to pay the credit-card company that $180 interest. You get to keep it. That $15 each month is money you can keep—it is your 18 percent return on your $1,000 investment in your debt. That kind of return on investment is unheard of these days.

NO MINIMUMS Investing in your debt imposes no minimums. For instance, if you have an extra dollar, you can invest it in your debt. This is not true of investing in the stock market. Most brokerages have minimum-purchase requirements, as do most mutual funds. It's not unusual for a mutual fund to require an opening purchase of $1,000 or more. Investing in mutual funds and the stock market almost always has conditions.

It makes so much sense, if you have any money to invest, to invest it in your unsecured debt until it is gone! Then what? Should you invest in your secured debts?

That's a question only you can answer. It is a conservative approach, but every benefit of investing in your unsecured debt transfers to your secured debt. Your "return on investment" will be less, however, since mortgage interest is typically less than interest charged on credit cards.

Still, every dollar you invest in your mortgage puts you that much closer to owning your home free and clear. Once paid, it's yours. No one will ever be able to take it from you, regardless of what happens to the economy or the stock market.

Money Is Not for Spending

It took me a long time to fully understand this profound truth: Money is not for spending. It is for managing first and then for spending. It takes courage to believe that, but when you do, the realization will profoundly change the way you think about and then manage your money.

Imagine this: It's Friday, a day you have come to know and love as cake day. You want cake, you love cake, and doggone it, you deserve to eat cake. You stop at the store and pick up the ingredients necessary to bake a cake.

The most bizarre thing happens on the way home. You can't wait. You begin eating the ingredients because you are so hungry for cake and simply cannot restrain yourself. You gulp a couple of eggs, chew up some butter and sugar, and down a load of flour and cocoa.

You pull into the driveway completely disgusted with yourself. You try to hide the evidence, but it's all over your face. But the worst part is that eating the cake was not nearly as satisfying as you'd dreamed it would be. It was, in fact, anything but enjoyable.

Now you feel ashamed and embarrassed. You conclude there's nothing you can do until the next cake day except suffer and beat yourself up for having been so incredibly foolish. And hope no one finds out.

An absurd analogy for sure, but it does illustrate the foolishness of eating food that has not yet been prepared. The very same ingredients that made you sick could have become a culinary masterpiece had you exposed them to a recipe. Those cake ingredients were not for eating—they were for preparing first and then for eating.

It is equally foolish and unsatisfying to spend money that has not first been managed. To manage money simply means to take full possession of it, to subject it to a specific plan and then direct it accordingly. It is a matter of creating a season of ownership between receiving and dispersing.

Managing money is a learned discipline, a conscious effort that produces gratification. When money flows into your life, you are responsible for what it does, where it goes, and how it performs. You are the boss. You can watch it drift away and out of your control, or you can manage it according to a formula, a plan—a specific "recipe" that you have developed and is a part of who you are.

It doesn't matter if you are a single parent struggling to survive with no outside help, or the CEO of a prosperous business—you need to know ahead of time exactly how you will manage every dime that flows into your life.

Certain mandatory elements must be part of your management system—elements like giving and saving. When you bring sanity and reason to the management of your income, feelings of dissatisfaction, worry, and hopelessness will quiet down. You will be driven to find and then plug the money leaks in your life.

A commitment to spending no more than you earn will become so important that you'll find yourself keeping track of where the money goes. Don't be surprised if you begin to reduce, reuse—even (gasp!) recycle—as a way of living within the plan you have developed.

So what is the best recipe for managing your money? It's simple: 10—10—80. Give away 10 percent, save 10 percent, and then live on 80 percent of your income. This formula works with any income, any situation, and any personality type.

No matter your situation—single, married, old, young; whether you're deeply in debt, unemployed, or at the top of your career—you need a system through which to process every dime that enters your life. Only then will you fully understand why money is not for spending. It is for managing first, and then for spending.

By the way, I have a killer chocolate cake recipe if you are interested.

My Life as a Frog

Frogs are not exactly the most intelligent creatures on the planet.

I have been told—you might have heard about this—if you try to pop a frog into a pot of boiling water, he'll jump out every time. That's pretty smart. But if you put the little fellow into a pot of cold water, set it on a low flame, and warm it up slowly, he'll sit back, relax, and let you cook him to death. That's really dumb.

The frog is so impressed by the nice, warm, cozy feeling, he doesn't pay attention to what's going on. Before he knows what hit him, *Bam!* Fresh frog soup.

I spent a lot of years as a frog. Oh, I was never so foolish as to make a single credit-card purchase for something really big or expensive like a boat or a car. Now that I think of it, I don't know that I've even heard of someone buying something with, say, a $10,000 price tag and swiping the plastic to pay for it. That's a boiling pot none of us could tolerate.

When I jumped into the pot, it was really cool—a terrific environment filled with freedom and options. My credit cards bridged that tiny gap between what we had and what we needed to enjoy the lifestyle we'd chosen. I don't even remember when the temperature began to rise, the process was so gradual.

I don't know exactly when it happened, but at some point our monthly credit purchases exceeded the amount we could repay within the grace period. Maybe I flinched the first time we "revolved," but I soon got used to the warming water.

By the time I was fully cooked, I'd accumulated more than $100,000 in unsecured debt, including credit cards, personal loans, debt-consolidation loans, and installment loans. Ouch! You have no idea how many times I've asked myself how in the world I could have let that happen. My only explanation is that it happened a little bit at a time—so gradually I didn't notice.

I didn't make unusually large, exotic purchases. I just overspent, consistently adding new debt to old debt and revolving all of it from month to month. I paid the interest and fees but rarely any principal.

I was forever on the lookout for new forms of credit, thinking that if I qualified, I could afford it. I was flattered by credit-card applications and credit-limit increases. I believed they made a statement about my character. I rationalized the situation by telling myself that even though we owed a lot, it could be a lot worse.

Like a frog I just sat there as the water got hotter and hotter and hotter.

Thankfully I did shed my amphibious nature and got out of a rolling boil, but not without a lot of, shall we say, *cooling down*. It took a full thirteen years to repair the mess.

Are things getting a little warm for you? You could be close to the scalding point and completely oblivious of the fact. Perhaps it's time to take your temperature. Here's a thermometer of telltale signs to determine if you're about to get cooked.

- You use a credit card to buy day-to-day necessities like food and gas.
- You pay only the minimum payment on your credit-card balance.
- You're behind in your payments.
- You frequently receive late notices and pay late fees.
- You're at or over the limit on your credit cards.
- You cringe when the phone rings.
- Your credit report stinks.
- You do not know how much you owe or what you spend on interest.

If things seem a little hotter than they should be, I suggest you perform a most unfroglike move: get out!

Ribbit.

Solving the Parent-Teen Crisis

They want independence and freedom. You want them to take responsibility for their actions.

They want decision-making power. You want them to make the right choices.

They want you to trust them. You want to hold the purse strings tightly.

They are struggling to break away. You cannot bear the thought of letting go.

Welcome to adolescence.

Today's teens are fortunate to be growing up in the most progressive and exciting time in history. That's the good news. The bad news is that the very culture that offers them the world is perpetuating a lie: you are entitled to have everything you want even if you don't have the money to pay for it.

Take a teenager with this attitude of entitlement, mix in his desire for independence, and stir in a generous dose of financial ignorance. Now expose the result to an already-stretched-to-the-limit household income, and you have the perfect recipe for parent-teen strife.

Not surprisingly, most conflicts between teens and parents find their roots in money issues. "No matter how much I give him, it's never enough. He spends it all on trinkets, CDs, clothes, and junk food," one parent told me recently. "And when I have to say no, he says I'm cheap and unfair. He thinks there is no end to my resources. We fight about money every day." What was a simple conflict over money erupted into a major breakdown in communication and trust between this mother and son.

So what's a family to do? Are teen-parent money conflicts inevitable? Must parents white-knuckle it through the teen years and hope everyone comes out okay at the other end? While this is an option to which many parents default, it's not an approach I would recommend. There is a better way.

While our two boys were still young, we recognized an alarming propensity toward narcissism, entitlement, and dissatisfaction. And why not? From the moment they were born, we did what came naturally. We overindulged them. They were still in single digits, and already it appeared our adorable children were turning into acquisitive ingrates. More wasn't enough. In other areas of life, we were diligently passing on to our boys the important values of responsibility, honesty, self-discipline, and faith. Failing so miserably in this matter of money had the effect of canceling out those other important life lessons.

As a part of my journey to financial recovery, we developed a simple kid-sized financial plan. In short, we assigned to each of our boys a portion of the family's financial resources to manage— an amount commensurate with each son's age, needs, and ability. We handed over fairly large sums of money to their discretion and control. They had to go through basic training; they had rules to obey about giving and saving. They had expenses to cover (we made a specific list of all the things we would no longer pay for), decisions to make, and consequences to suffer. What they didn't know was that their monthly "salary" wasn't a new expense for us—it was the money that we would have spent on them anyway and that we were shelling out daily. Our promise to them was that as long as they gave away 10 percent and saved 10 percent, we would not criticize their decisions, nor would we bail them out. There would be no loans, no advances.

From the day the plan went into effect, the change was remarkable, if not miraculous. Gratitude and appreciation replaced attitudes of entitlement. They could hardly believe we'd trust them with "so much money." In the beginning they made some foolish blunders, but they were small and harmless. In the end they became amazing savers. They taught *themselves* how to live frugally. Money conflicts vanished as if overnight.

No doubt, the letting-go part of parenting isn't easy. But we can make the process easier and more enjoyable if we keep this thought uppermost: God's plan is for children to grow wings and fly away. Our job as parents is to prepare them for the flight. Building financial confidence in your kids is one important way you can help them fly high above the turbulence with grace and endurance.

You Call *This* Peace on Earth?

The trouble with Christmas is not that it's become over-commercialized—tell me what part of our lives hasn't? The trouble with Christmas is that we allow it to get the better of us. We treat it as a contest or final examination rather than a time of rest, reflection, and joy.

In our fantasies, Christmas comes into our lives like a horse-drawn sleigh, decorated with holly, pine boughs, and bells. As it glides to our doorstep, we're invited to climb aboard as we are handed the reins to the mighty team of Clydesdales. As we direct this thing of beauty through the crisp, sparkling holidays, the only sounds we hear are the clippety-clop of horses' hooves and the jingling of sleigh bells. The sights and sounds are breathtaking. We visit friends and loved ones, exchange perfect gifts, indulge in warm and meaningful conversations; grateful children frolic in the snow amazed by the generosity of the season.

We sing familiar carols, reflect on childhood memories, and rest more than we work. Every night we sit around the fireplace sipping hot cider. Our bodies and souls are refreshed as we arrive at Christmas Day with grateful hearts.

The day is spent enjoying sumptuous food and basking in the joy of being together with friends and relatives. We participate in family traditions that bring us more joy and satisfaction than we ever thought possible.

In reality, Christmas comes roaring into our lives like an eighteen-wheeled, supercharged, nitrous-burning, straight-six, diesel-powered, self-propelled juggernaut of a Big Rig. It pulls up, yells for us to get on board, and instructs us to find a seat in the rear. We hang on for dear life, knowing we'll have no say on how this thing will get us to where we have to be in less than a month. The number of Shopping Days Left till Christmas blinks in headache-inducing neon lights. It doesn't take long to realize this is going to be some kind of a ride.

The thirty days between Thanksgiving and Christmas become a blur as we tear through town feeling obligated to stop at every turn to decorate, shop, clean, cook, bake, wrap, send, and referee. The rig is programmed to go faster and faster because we have so little time and so many miles to cover before the journey's end.

As hard as we try to ignore it, this machine needs fuel and lots of it—and credit cards have become the combustible of choice. We are terrified at how often we need to refuel.

We find little time to sleep with so many mandatory parties, pageants, and projects. We feel ourselves being consumed by guilt and obligation and attempt to counteract those feelings by charging (we hope it's deferred billing) bigger and better gifts and buying the approval and adoration of parents and children by taking on the role of Christmas Magician.

As we enter the final laps, we give up trying to conserve on the fuel because the only thing that matters is getting there before midnight on Christmas Eve. At the eleventh hour, we screech across the finish line. Our bodies exhausted and our spirits spent, we are thrown out into our homes as Big Rig screams out of our lives, and none too soon.

But instead of hearing the lovely strains of "May your days be merry and bright . . ." as the rig disappears into the distance, we hear only the threat "I'll Be Back!"

No doubt about it, celebrating Christmas in the 1990s is a far cry from what it was even thirty years ago, thanks to the evolution of consumer credit. No longer must we concern ourselves with whether there's enough money to have and do all that our hearts desire. Credit-card companies have made it quite socially accept-able to have it all whether we can afford it or not. Little by little we've allowed ourselves to have what we want now and worry about paying for it later.

The more we have, the more we want, and the more we get, the more we need to feel satisfied. It seems that no matter how fantastic Christmas was last year, we are compelled to make it even bigger and better this year.

Fuel! Holiday extravagance comes down to a matter of fuel, and plastic has become the fuel of choice when it comes to Christ-mas in America. The cost is staggering.

How staggering? Check this out: in the twenty-six days be-tween Thanksgiving and Christmas 1996, American consumers charged a whopping $131.4 billion dollars on their credit cards—an all-time high and up 13 percent from the previous year. While some of these charges were repaid within the grace periods, more than $70 billion went on to become revolving debt—plunging those credit-card holders who can least afford it into even deeper financial bondage.

When it's all said and done, it seems the entire gift-giving process—which is what really started all of this in the first place—has all but become divorced from the actual impulse, from the love or the kindness. It's just shopping; it's just money; it's just crossing names off lists and moving on.

I recall that when I was a child, my dad used to compare his childhood Christmases to ours. His "I was lucky to get an orange and a few nuts for Christmas" was as much a tradition as anything around our house. And his point? To contrast how overindulged we were with how deprived he was. I rolled my eyes then, but every now and again the simplicity of such a time does hold a certain charm.

Look, I'm not suggesting that we return to the piece-of-citrus-and-a-couple-of-pecans standard. Nor am I suggesting that we can transform our Big Rig kind of holidays into charming carefree sleigh rides through the season. What I am suggesting is that it is possible to stand back, evaluate, and then come up with a plan where our expectations are realistic, our efforts provide satisfaction, and everything is paid in full.

Stop Whining!

To me, the mother of two young world-class whiners, the behavior-modification techniques described in the little book appeared too simple to be taken seriously. In desperation, however, I decided to give the antiwhining program my best shot.

DAY 1: Whenever one of the boys whined, I did exactly as the book prescribed. I got down to his level, looked him straight in the eye, and said in a firm-yet-gentle manner, "Stop whining! I cannot listen to you when you whine because it gives me a headache."

Next, I imitated what he said and the way he said it, right down to his nasally, high-pitched, singsong tone. Then I restated in a grown-up voice what he said, using a better choice of words and required him to repeat it without whining, blaming, or complaining.

I did this no less than 397 times before bedtime on day 1.

DAY 2: The second day was similar to the first, except that after my demonstration of the correct way to communicate, I had to turn away and ignore the child until on his own he restated his need or situation without whining, blaming, or complaining.

DAY 3: This day's instructions were challenging if not severe: if either boy whined, I was to ignore him completely as if he were invisible. They would get my attention only when they did not whine. This new behavior was more difficult for me than for them. Always before, I had rewarded their whining with my attention and an immediate response. That had to stop. From now on they would be rewarded with attention only when they did not whine—or it was a matter of life and death.

The program worked like magic. In just three days our boys became nonwhiners just as the book promised. It was not so, however, for their mother.

I had my own style of whining. It was adult-sized and somewhat more socially acceptable, mainly because no one could hear it. I whined in my thoughts and attitudes.

We don't make enough money; I want everything everyone else has; I don't want to wait—I want it right now! I work hard, and I deserve it!

I whined my way into fancy new cars and things like a mink jacket. I wanted to be part of the jet set, where that kind of luxury was standard. I whined until I got what I wanted and then whined about our miserable financial condition. Whine, whine, whine, whine, whine.

Even on the road to financial recovery, I whined, blamed, and complained: *It's too hard; I want to be a stay-at-home mom; it's just not fair; I'm tired of waiting; I just can't take this anymore; no one else has it this rough.*

One day, out of complete and utter frustration with myself and recalling those sessions with my kids years before, I sat myself down and looked myself straight in the eye. *Stop whining! I cannot listen to you when you whine because it gives me a headache.*

I went on to repeat some of my loathsome whining, and that

shocked me nearly to death. Do I really sound like *that?* Treatment was clear: I had to kick into tough love mode and completely ignore myself when I whined. I could not pay attention to myself when I blamed, complained, or whined.

What an experience. Holding up a mirror to reflect back my attitudes and behavior did not create a pretty picture. No wonder I couldn't shake my sense of misery. As long as I was willing to see myself as the victim of my circumstances, I was not fully responsible—it wasn't my fault. And as long as I rewarded myself with sympathy and attention, I just kept whining, blaming, and complaining.

The result was fairly astounding. In a short time, I too became a nonwhiner.

So tell me. Are you a whiner? Are you into blaming and complaining? Perhaps you're still carrying on about the ugly divorce, those huge medical bills, your youthful ignorance, the sudden unemployment, and totally unfair circumstances that were not your fault.

Perhaps you're whining about all the reasons getting a job is an impossibility and filing for bankruptcy is the only way out.

I have a suggestion. Sit yourself down, look yourself straight in the eye, and say: *Stop whining! I cannot listen to you when you whine because it gives me a headache.* Refuse to listen to that anymore. Do not reward yourself with sympathy and attention when you whine, blame, and complain. And stop feeling sorry for yourself.

As long as you see yourself as a victim, things will not change. You will never fix your problems while you blame others for your circumstances. Whatever your situation, regardless of the details, you are accountable. You are responsible.

You can either give in to your circumstances or rise above

them. You can remain in your misery or climb out of that rut and look around.

You can reward your whining, blaming, and self-pity with your full attention, or you can completely ignore yourself when you slip into that debilitating mode.

You can choose thoughts that support your misery or thoughts that will lead you to action and a solution.

You can keep living in denial, or you can find the courage to face the truth.

You can dig your pit of despair a little deeper, or you can make the commitment to do whatever it takes to turn your financial life around.

The choice is yours.

The Wisdom to Decide

Usually I try to avoid making broad generalizations. I have, however, come to the unavoidable conclusion that everyone has gone nuts. Okay, maybe not everyone. But almost everyone.

On what do I base this conclusion? Last Christmas we (not you and me, of course . . . I use the royal "we") spent 4 percent of our annual incomes, or $1,000 per person, on Christmas gifts!

Of course we didn't actually "spend" that much, if "spend" indeed means to pay out money. We actually spent far less than that, but made up the shortfall with our handy-dandy credit cards. Now isn't that a brilliant idea? We don't have the money now, but of course we'll have it—plus interest—next month and the next month and the next and on and on.

So let's take a closer look at what really happened.

We pledged money we didn't have yet (maybe still don't) to

pay for stuff we can't remember anymore. And what have we been concentrating on in the months since? Worrying ourselves half-sick over too-much-month-too-little-money, searching desperately for debt-consolidation loans, signing up for credit counseling, even applying for home-equity loans to get rid of all those high-rate credit-card balances.

And when all the holiday hype calms down, we enter the new year tenaciously committed to paring down, uncluttering, dejunking, slogging through, and ridding ourselves of all the extraneous stuff that weighs us down, steals our time, and stifles our joy. The brutal truth is that much of the stuff that now clutters our lives was at one time wrapped and sitting under the Christmas tree.

See what I mean? We're crazy.

So here we are, halfway through the eleven-month downtime that separates our annual spending orgies. The days are long and lazy. It's the perfect time to simply sit back and think. And decide. Decide what next Christmas will be.

Who will be in charge? Will it be us or big-bucks credit-card companies? Will we give in to the pressures around us or take charge and follow our good sense?

Our lives are the sum total of the decisions we make. Making unwise decisions increases the likelihood our lives will turn out badly. Making good decisions contributes enormously to effective, happy, and fulfilled living.

America's beloved poet Robert Frost expressed the significance of decisions in his poem "The Road Not Taken":

> *Two roads diverged in a yellow wood,*
> *And sorry I could not travel both*
> *And be one traveler, long I stood*

And looked down one as far as I could
To where it bent in the undergrowth;

Then took the other, . . .
. . . .
Oh, I kept the first for another day!
Yet knowing how way leads on to way,
I doubted if I should ever come back.

I shall be telling this with a sigh
Somewhere ages and ages hence:
Two roads diverged in a wood, and I—
I took the one less traveled by,
And that has made all the difference.

Life is a series of forks in the road. One decision leads to another. Is it a wise decision or one that will be destructive? Does it lead to higher ground or to a valley of despair? Does it lead to something better and more fulfilling? Or does it set us up for eventual defeat, steady decline, and self-destruction?

It takes wisdom to make good decisions. Wisdom is not a rare commodity reserved for an elite few. Wisdom is available to all who seek truth and knowledge.

So here we stand at yet another fork in the road. Destination: Holidays 2001.

The one path is posted "Debt-free." It's the less-traveled, slower route, narrow and uphill. But at the destination are joy, simplicity, satisfaction, and a trophy engraved "Paid-in-full."

The other road is "Convenience," a very tempting, ultramodern highway paved with easy credit. Taking this high-tech option means effortless travel. But the high occurrence of holiday overindulgence, dissatisfaction, and stress leaves many travelers filled with guilt, regret, and fear. There is no trophy for reaching this destination, only a miserable monthly reminder of the high cost of convenience.

Which road will you take? That decision will make all the difference.

Appendix B
Fifty Fabulous Ideas
from Folks like You

1. Do not pay for an unlisted phone number (also referred to as "nonpublished" in some areas). The fee for unlisted service costs anywhere from $1 to $3 a month. If for security and privacy reasons you choose not to let your name be published in the phone book and given out by directory operators, use your pet's name or the middle name of one of your children instead. Your security will not be compromised because if someone calls for your pet, you'll know immediately that it is probably not someone you care to speak with.—B. M., New Jersey

2. Instead of throwing away a pair of pantyhose with a run in one leg, I wait for a second pair in the same shade to run, also in one leg. Then I simply cut off the "injured" legs just below the crotch. I wear both one-legged pantyhose at the same time with a newly created girdle formed by

wearing both panty parts of the hose. I've saved big bucks doing this!—K. M., New York

3. I never spend dimes. By adopting a personal attitude that the only thing I can do with dimes is save them, I consistently add $50 to $100 a year to my savings account—just in dimes!—R. D., Illinois

4. I discovered a great tip quite by accident. Every morning my husband poured the Efferdent water in which his false teeth had been soaking overnight in the toilet bowl. After a while I noticed that it cleaned the bowl so well that I no longer had to do heavy scrubbing with the weekly toilet cleaning.—M. B., Michigan

5. My mother colors her gray hair, but she buys Just For Men. It is half the cost and lasts twice as long as what she was using previously. It beats buying the brands available for women, which are expensive and tend to give too much product for her short hair.—T. C., Georgia

6. Lint recently escaped my dryer filter and stuck to my pants instead. I grabbed the closest item I could find to try to brush away the lint. It happened to be a used Cling Free dryer sheet out of the wastebasket. I just ran it over the lint, and to my amazement all of the lint came right off. No more expensive lint-remover rollers for me.—P. A. F., California

7. Three scales worth their weight in gold: a 25-pound scale in the laundry room so wash loads are right—not too much and not too little; a 5-pound scale in the kitchen to measure food portions for serving, freezing, and storing; and a 300-pound scale for weight control. The kitchen scale will also serve to weigh mail. No more wasting postage stamps to make sure you've used enough. You will know.—A. J., Illinois

8. Buy a three-pack of all-cotton white T-shirts to use as pajamas or beach cover-ups for small children. I buy a size large enough that the bottom edge is just below the knees.—J. D., Florida

9. To keep milk fresh longer, add a pinch of salt when it is first opened. It doubles the useful shelf life.—E. G., Florida

10. When I get the urge to purchase a new book, I call my library first. If it isn't in circulation, I request they order it. Nine times out of ten the library will decide to add it to their shelves. Within a few weeks, it arrives and I enjoy the book for free.—L. N., Connecticut

11. Most physicians are generously supplied with medication samples (also known as "stock bottles") by pharmaceutical companies. Always ask for a supply of these samples when your doctor prescribes medication. Doctors can even write a prescription for a stock bottle to be filled at the pharmacy for patients unable to afford the prescription. Asking for sufficient samples to make sure the medication is right is especially wise. There's nothing more frustrating than spending a fortune on an expensive prescription only to find out that you're allergic to it or that it is not effective. Additionally, the Pharmaceutical Manufacturer's Association of America has a directory of programs for those who cannot afford prescription drugs. Call 1-800-PMA-INFO to determine if you might qualify.—S. Mc., Pennsylvania

12. My favorite use for an empty thirty-five-millimeter film canister is as a spaghetti measurer. Stack uncooked spaghetti into a canister. A full canister makes spaghetti for two—no waste, no guessing. I recently saw a spaghetti

measurer in a kitchen shop with a $4.95 price tag. I chuckled knowing mine was free!—M. S., Wyoming

13. Use "marine" paint for the window trim in bathrooms if there is contact with water. I also use this paint on patio furniture and any other place that gets a lot of moisture. Marine paint is specially formulated to hold up well under wet conditions. This kind of specialty paint does cost a little more, but it's worth it because it is so durable. —D. I., North Carolina

14. I use a no-tears baby shampoo to remove eye makeup. I learned this from an ophthalmologist I worked for. We encouraged our contact lens wearers to do this to reduce protein buildup on their lenses. Apply with a Q-Tip in a brushing motion while holding eyelid taut.—M. G., Texas

15. Here's a cheap, fun indoor activity for preschoolers. I pour coarse cornmeal (polenta) into roasting pans to make "sandboxes." The kids play happily for a long time with their little cars and people. The cleanup is pretty simple with a minivacuum. These kinds of pans are readily available at yard sales. I keep a large container of cornmeal (cheap!) on hand just for this purpose.—L. C., California

16. Put cooking oil in a clean, plastic spray bottle. This is much cheaper than buying oil in a spray can, and you can use the exact type of oil you want.—L. M., Pennsylvania

17. I use Rit Dye a lot, especially when redecorating. I dyed my bedroom curtains from peach to wine when we painted the room mauve. They turned out beautifully. Six years ago, I dyed my bathroom rugs from peach to green and now plan to change them to wine to match the new de-

cor. (I never throw bathroom rugs in the dryer, since they have rubber backing. I believe this has prolonged their life.) Rit Dye can be found in all kinds of stores for under $2 a box. Follow directions carefully.—K. C., Illinois

18. I mix one part cornstarch to one part bath powder (my favorite is baby powder, but any kind will do), put the mixture in a pretty container, and add a nice fluffy powder puff. This extends the bath powder tremendously and feels great on the skin. People who are sensitive to fragrances could leave out the scented powder and just use cornstarch. It makes a good bath powder all by itself. I do the same thing with body lotions. I pick a favorite scent, buy a bottle of inexpensive, fragrance-free lotion, and add an equal amount of the scented lotion. Makes my favorite last twice as long.—M. H., Illinois

19. Orvus Horse Shampoo (available in pet stores) made my wool blend holiday sweater look better than new and eliminated the "scratchiness." My favorite elegant sweater with stones and silver threads was looking pretty tacky; it had really lost its luster. The dry cleaner refused to touch it. A lady who teaches quilting classes recommends this shampoo for laundering quilts and other fine things. It sounded crazy to me, but I figured I didn't have much more to lose. I was astonished at the results. Hint: use only about one tablespoon horse shampoo to a sink full of water.— J. M., Washington

20. I'm a major cookie-baker and enjoy lining my cookie sheets with parchment paper. I was paying $4.75 (or about 20¢ for enough for one batch) a roll for the stuff at a kitchen specialty store. That was before I began living by *Cheapskate Monthly*! I asked around, and sure enough the

local bakery counter will sell me parchment paper for just 2¢ per extra-large sheet (big enough for two of my cookie sheets). What savings!—N. B., Kansas

21. When my automatic coffeemaker with a timer died recently, I was aghast at what a new one would cost. Here's my cheaper, but better, solution: I bought a less-expensive model without a timer and an automatic timer device sold at a hardware store (normally used to turn lamps off and on automatically). I plugged my new coffeemaker into the timer. It works perfectly!—J. S., Massachusetts

22. Ashes from a wood-burning stove or fireplace make wonderful fertilizer for rosebushes.—K. E., Texas

23. Don't throw away all of your used laundry-softener sheets. When you have an impossible-to-clean casserole dish or pot, toss one or two of the used sheets into the pan, fill it with hot water, and *presto!* In twenty minutes, it wipes clean. No scrubbing needed. I store mine in an empty tissue box.—S. H., Florida

24. Here's the jewelry cleaner professional stores use: Mix equal amounts of household ammonia and water. It's cheap, it works, and it's the best.—C. F., Washington

25. I make an occasional trip to the newspaper in my area and buy newsprint roll-ends for about $1.50. There is always a lot of paper left on the rolls, and it is useful for wrapping gifts (can be self-decorated in limitless ways), for stuffing packages to be mailed, and as "art" paper for murals, fingerpainting, and crayoning. I donate rolls to the local elementary school, where they're used for all kinds of projects.—H. H., Massachusetts

26. Use Murphy's Oil Soap (available in grocery stores in the cleaning-product section) on your pet's dry, itchy, or flea-allergic skin. It is gentle and all-vegetable. Especially

good for shar-peis with all of their skin problems. For an effective flea dip, boil orange and lemon peels in water. Cool and use for pet rinse or dip. Smells nice and fresh. You can also slice citrus and rub the fruit into the dog's fur. The bugs will keel over from the smell.—K. H., California

27. Are your children's marking pens starting to dry out? Dip the tip of the marker in water for about ten seconds. Dry excess water, and you have just extended the life of the markers.—L. P., Illinois

28. The next time one of your leather belts wears out, don't throw it away. It will make a great collar for your pet. Just cut it down to size and punch a new hole.—J. F., New York

29. Tired of throwing out celery that's lost its crisp and crunch? Cut the bottom stem off and separate the stalks. Fill a pan that is deep enough to cover the celery with cold water and stir in three-quarters of a cup of cup granulated sugar. Let the celery soak for four or five hours. Drain it well and refrigerate it.—V. E., Colorado

30. Here's a recipe for inexpensive bubble bath: Mix 2 cups of vegetable oil, 2 tablespoons of shampoo, and 10 drops of perfume (optional). Beat it at high speed for two or three minutes to emulsify it. Keep it in a tightly closed bottle. Use about 3 tablespoons in each bath.—L. M., Pennsylvania

31. Another good window cleaner: 1 cup of rubbing alcohol, 1 cup of household ammonia, 1 cup of distilled water. Put the mixture in a spray bottle and label it. I like this better than the vinegar version.—C. R., Iowa

32. I give myself $100-a-month allowance. I carry only $40 with me and put the remaining $60 in an envelope. Many times at the end of the month I still have most of the

$60 left and use it to buy Texaco, Inc., stock (now Chevron Texaco), which can be purchased directly from the company with an initial purchase of $250 and subsequent purchases of only $50. There are no brokerage fees, and all dividends are reinvested. Chevron Texaco's shareholder's services can be contacted at 800-522-6645.—L. C. R., Michigan

33. I enjoy going out for lunch on the days I work but usually forget to write down how much I spend and end up spending way too much. But I've discovered something that works great for me: On Monday I take $25 cash and put it in an envelope, to be used only for my lunches. If it's gone before Friday, I have to take my lunch. This has really helped me to keep control of my finances without feeling deprived.—D. P., Florida

34. Don't throw out that old silver chest designed to store silverware and prevent tarnishing. It makes a wonderful jewelry box. Earrings clip to the band designed to hold knives. Chains, rings, and brooches fit nicely in the open spaces, and because of the specially treated material that lines this type of chest, nothing will tarnish.—A. B., Illinois

35. To prolong the life of swimsuits that are exposed to harsh chlorine, I purchase chlorine remover (either liquid or tablets) that is manufactured for removing chlorine from fish tanks. This product can be found in any pet-supply store. I add a few drops of the liquid to a pail of cold water, pop the suits in when we're done swimming, and follow up with a cold tap water rinse.—D. V. L., Wisconsin

36. To extend the useful life of dry staples—such as flour, meal, grits, pastas, and rice—pop in a couple of bay leaves. This won't affect the taste, but it prevents pesky bugs from ruining these products before they can be consumed.—C. G., Florida

37. Here's great weed killer you can make for less than $2 a gallon. Dissolve 1 pound of table salt in 1 gallon of white vinegar (5 percent acidity is ideal). Add a few drops of liquid dishwashing detergent (this helps plant material absorb the liquid). Label it and keep it out of reach of children. Use it in an ordinary spray bottle. This nontoxic formula acts as a temporary soil sterilizer, so don't spray near roots of trees, shrubs, or plants you want to keep. I find it especially effective on my gravel driveway. I zap the weeds as they begin to appear.—V. W., Colorado

38. As a stay-at-home mom who loves to cook, here's how I earn money. I prepare dinner meals for two families in my neighborhood. Each family pays me from $8 to $10 per meal. The money I collect pays for all of the food for them and for my family. It's just as easy to cook for two as for twelve. I deliver home-style dinners to the houses just before the families arrive home for the evening. This frees them up to spend time with their kids, I receive gratification from cooking, and my family eats for free. I use lots of coupons and always create the week's menus from the weekly sale ads the stores place in my Thursday newspaper.— A. F., California

39. If you are planning a wedding, contact a cake-decorating class. You can coordinate with them to get a cake at an amazing price. I've done it.—M. C., California

40. Here's how to make an effective, inexpensive heating pad. Take a clean sock (a man's tube sock with no holes works best). Fill it halfway with about five cups of raw regular white rice. Tie a knot in the top. Warm it in a microwave on high at thirty-second intervals until the desired heat is reached. This heating device will stay in good shape as long as it does not get wet. I've been using the same one

for more than a year. I learned this trick when I was in the hospital for a neck injury. This heating pad conforms well and is perfect for headaches, earaches, backaches, neck aches, cramps—anything that would call for a heating pad. —K. S., Alabama

41. We recently moved into an area where the water has a very high iron content. In less than six months, this discolored the inside of a brand-new dishwasher and even the edges of some of my dishes. I tried bleach, baking soda, vinegar, Comet, and any other cleanser I could find. Finally I complained to the builder. He recommended I try Tang Breakfast Drink! I ran an empty cycle and filled the soap dispensers with the powdered mix (it has to be Tang). The stains vanished. It is truly amazing. I have no idea why it works, but who cares? It does.—K. S., Washington

42. When a good friend was expecting her fourth child, I hosted a rather unusual baby shower for her. Instead of the usual baby gifts, the invitations invited guests to bring a frozen dish, casserole, dessert, etc., for the guest of honor's freezer. They were also requested to bring a copy of the rec-ipe. We presented her with a "cookbook" (using a photo al-bum) along with a freezer full of food. It was fun and inexpensive and gave my friend precious time to spend with the new baby instead of in the kitchen.—J. S., Massachusetts

43. To remove residue buildup on your hair and make it shiny and bouncy, mix one tablespoon of dry baking soda with the amount of shampoo you normally use for one hair washing. Repeat this process about once a month. This is a cheap substitute for expensive commercial products that do the same thing.—S. H., Washington

44. Stop leaking ice-cream cones and their result-
ant disasters by placing a marshmallow in the bottom of
the cone before loading on the ice cream.—L. F.,
New York

45. Another use for dryer sheets: Use these sheets (new
or used) as interfacing when appliquéing a quilt (the layer
between the cutout and the quilt top). This keeps the quilt
fresher longer between washings and airings, adds incredibly lightweight insulation, and extends the life of the quilt.
—C. A., Massachusetts

46. To clean the inside of a glass thermos bottle, place
an Efferdent denture cleaning tablet in it, fill it with warm
water, and allow it to sit overnight.—C. S., Arkansas

47. I recently painted a bathroom and my kids' bed-
rooms for less than $20. I bought high-quality "mistinted"
paint at a local home improvement center for just $3 a gal-
lon and 50c per quart. The colors are super, and my kids
loved it. Most hardware stores have bins of these kinds of
"goofs" at near-giveaway prices.—S. G., Iowa

48. A kitchen accident left my white range top with an
ugly chip in the porcelain. An estimate of $100 to repair
the porcelain encouraged me to find some cheaper alternative. Liquid Paper (correction fluid from a stationery store)
to the rescue! I gave it a try and to my amazement found it
covered the spot and lasts a long time. I simply reapply it
every year or so. It looks great!—B. A., Nebraska

49. If you have more time than money and need a new
lawn, visit your local sod farm and purchase their "scraps,"
which are the odd-sized roll ends. You will have to patch
them together, which takes time, but you can pick up these
odd pieces at a tremendous savings.—D. D., Colorado

50. In discussing the price of medication with my doctor, we decided that if I bought the one-hundred-milligram tablet and broke it in two where it is scored, I could get my prescribed fifty-milligram dosage and the second month's medication for just a few dollars more.—S. I., Kansas

WHAT IS
CHEAPSKATE MONTHLY?

Cheapskate Monthly is a twelve-page newsletter published twelve times a year, dedicated to helping those who are struggling to live within their means to find practical and realistic solutions to their financial problems. *Cheapskate Monthly* provides hope, encouragement, inspiration, and motivation to individuals who are committed to financially responsible and debt-free living and provides the highest-quality information and resources possible in a format exclusive of paid advertising. You will find *Cheapskate Monthly* filled with tips, humor, and great information to help you stretch those dollars till they scream!

(please turn the page)

How to Subscribe to *Cheapskate Monthly*

For print version, send check or money order for $22.95 to:

Cheapskate Monthly

P.O. Box 2135

Paramount, CA 90723-8135

(800) 550-3502

On-line version is available for $24.00. Go to

http://www.cheapskatemonthly.com

(Please call for Canadian and foreign rates.)

Special Offer from *Cheapskate Monthly*

Enclose this original coupon with your check or money order, and your one-year subscription to *Cheapskate Monthly* will be automatically extended for an additional three months. That's fifteen months for the price of twelve. Such a deal, considering $22.95 for twelve full issues is already CHEAP!

(Subscription rate subject to change without notice.)